Managing Return
on Investment

Managing Return on Investment

Implications for Pricing, Volume, and Funds Flow

George E. Manners, Jr.
Clemson University

Joseph G. Louderback III
Rensselaer Polytechnic Institute

LexingtonBooks
D.C. Heath and Company
Lexington, Massachusetts
Toronto

Library of Congress Cataloging in Publication Data

Manners, George E., 1943–
  Managing return on investment.

  Includes index.
  1. Capital investments—Evaluation. I. Louderback, Joseph G.
II. Title. III. Title: Return on investment.
HG4028.C4M18   658.1'5   80–8817
ISBN 0–669–04383–4   AACR2

Copyright © 1981 by D.C. Heath and Company

Published simultaneously in Canada

Printed in the United States of America

International Standard Book Number: 0–669–04383–4

Library of Congress Catalog Card Number: 80–8817

Contents

List of Figures

List of Tables

Preface and Acknowledgments

Many managers consider rate of return a valuable tool in analyzing courses of action. Alfred P. Sloan has said that rate of return is the best financial principle available as a guide and "objective aid to business judgment."[1]

This book is for managers who use return on investment (ROI), or who would like to, in making decisions regarding price, volume, investment, and a host of other factors like credit terms and inventory policy. Managers who use ROI for evaluating performance, or who are themselves so evaluated, will also benefit from this book. More specifically, our intended audience includes the following:

1. General managers who have profit and investment responsibility at both the divisional and corporate levels.
2. Staff people attached to such managers.
3. Financial managers, including controllers of divisions or corporations and their staffs.
4. Marketing managers, especially those empowered to make decisions about prices, credit terms, and discounts.
5. Management consultants, especially those who concentrate on operational aspects of management as well as on financial aspects.
6. Management advisory partners and principals of CPA firms with active Management Advisory Services divisions.

Our objectives are limited but important. The principal one is to present a model that managers can *use*. Accordingly, we present a model that is comprehensive, easily adapted to different organizations, and understandable. Moreover, the model requires no information that is not readily available from the accounting system of almost any firm—small, medium, or large. Essentially, the model requires information about cost behavior and turnovers of current assets and liabilities. It is important to note that we do not work with exotic mathematical formulations of demand curves or market-share models. We provide an approach to evaluating alternatives based on their expected ROIs, profits, and cash flows. Because the model is comprehensive, it permits quick determination of profit and cash-flow consequences of actions.

Most of the literature for practicing managers, as opposed to the academic literature, is not analytical. It does not show how the manager can take advantage of information that is usually available, and it does not link the important factors together. To cite a single example, the widely used "margin-times-turnover" model of ROI assumes, unrealistically, that the two factors are independent. In other words, managers usually must perform a series of iterations by making educated guesses until they arrive at a reasonably close answer. Given the widespread use of target ROI, it is surprising that such naive techniques are so well accepted.

At the other extreme lie the corporate (or divisional) simulators of varying degrees of sophistication and utility. Their one common element is cost—very high cost. These simulators allow managers to experiment with different strategies, but they may be neither flexible enough to accommodate particular conditions nor useful for the day-to-day analyses and decisions that managers must make.

We begin with a method of determining how to set a target ROI to achieve corporate objectives subject to existing constraints, and then we move to the basic ROI model. The model is used principally to answer three types of questions:

1. What ROI (as well as profit, investment, and cash flow) can we expect if our operations go according to plan?
2. More importantly, what must we do in the way of price, volume, turnover of inventory, and so forth, in order to achieve our target ROI?
3. What tradeoffs might we make to maintain or better our ROI? (For example, if we tighten credit terms, how much volume can we afford to lose without reducing ROI?)

A subsidiary benefit of the model is that, in the words of a chief executive officer (CEO) who has seen the material, "It's a great way to spot BS." One function of managers is to evaluate proposals. The model is helpful in evaluating proposed courses of action because it permits the manager to say, for example, "If we go ahead with what you propose, we shall have to increase our volume by 30 percent to maintain our ROI."

Essentially, our approach focuses on an analysis of the interplay of the factors that determine ROI. We are not concerned with the general aspects of, say, pricing, that include the effects of advertising and other elements. Instead, we look at pricing (for example) with the purpose of determining whether or not a particular price will give a target ROI and, if not, what price will.

We have tried to present a balanced view, but we think that our backgrounds in finance and accounting color much of our analysis. The careful reader will soon see that we emphasize the objective, reasonably determinable aspects of decisions and strategies. "What will it cost us?" is a recurring question. We pay more attention to the hard data than to the softer, more qualitative impressions. We do not deny the significance of this soft side of management; we do think, however, that in most cases hard analysis is necessary for better decisions and strategies.

Chapter 1 describes a method for setting a target ROI for the operating units of the firm. It provides one way for corporate managers to relate various corporate goals and constraints to an operating target.

Chapter 2 presents the basic ROI model that serves to guide the rest of the book. It defines terms; identifies the types of information required (all of which, again, come from the accounting system); and shows the advantages of using ROI, instead of just profit, as a decision criterion. It shows how ordinary cost-volume-profit analysis can be enhanced through its integration with the behavior of current assets. It also introduces a hypothetical manufacturing division, which we use throughout for illustration.

Chapter 3 shows how to set prices that will yield a target ROI, provided that managers have correctly estimated the values of the important variables, especially volume. It shows the effects of target pricing on a number of items of interest, including revenue, assets (total and individual), and cash requirements. It develops relationships between price and volume that should be helpful in assessing pricing strategies. Finally, the chapter integrates the popular concept of "pricing on the learning curve" with the target-ROI approach. One interesting point developed in chapter 3 is that the pursuit of market share through lower prices is a very costly strategy unless it is *very* successful.

Chapter 4 describes how to maintain ROI by changing prices in the face of changes in costs and turnovers. The chapter also treats tradeoffs and policy considerations, as well as the important topic that we call *incremental pricing*—that is, pricing sales to be made outside regular channels (for example, exports, private brands, and intrafirm transfers).

Chapter 5 looks at volume: how it affects ROI, how the firm must increase it to maintain ROI in the face of increasing costs and other unfavorable events, and how firms can trade volume off against other factors like credit terms and inventory policy.

Chapter 6 deals with investment. We do not use discounted-cash-flow analysis. We assume that managers use it in making capital investment decisions, but our concern is with book ROI. Again, we relate changes in investment to required changes in price, volume, and other factors. These relationships are extremely useful in the articulation of policy statements such as, "For each dollar we invest in new distribution facilities, we require at least 100 units of new volume in order to maintain ROI."

In developing and stating our results, we employ a good many formulas and equations, which we believe are essential to an understanding of the basic model and of its uses in decision making. Even the top-level corporate manager will want to try out some of these formulas, using company data.

The world of consulting and of books for business people is replete with exhibits, graphs, and tables showing how something is related to something else. Often, it is impossible to tell whether or not the results are plausible because there is no simple way to verify them. This situation can be very messy for the person who wishes to see how to apply the results to a particular situation. Of course, we understand that many managers do not wish to go through numerous equations in order to determine whether or not a particular one might be suitable for their own operations or, perhaps, for modification by a staff member of moderate quantitative talent.

Accordingly, readers may skim lightly over formulas and equations without losing continuity or understanding, particularly on a first reading. The models and methods of analysis are devices intended to help the reader picture his or her own operations.

Having said all of this, we hasten to add that there are no higher mathematics in the text. We use a good deal of algebra, but no calculus. More importantly, we repeat that we use only data that are readily available from the firm's accounting system. There are no demand curves, market-share models, probabilistic equations, functions to be optimized, or other exotica. We simply seek to relate industry's most commonly used operational construct (ROI) to a set of income and asset variables that is understandable and practical in a wide range of situations.

We wish to express our appreciation to a number of individuals for their stimulation and assistance in developing the material in this book. Special thanks go to George Manners, Sr., of Georgia State University for his continuous support and encouragement of our ideas. Dr. Daniel Orne of Norton Corporation; Dr. Joseph Steger of Colt Industries; Mr. G. Robert Tod of CML Group, Inc.; and Dr. Donald Jewell of Georgia State University took time out of their busy schedules to review our material and provide valuable feedback. We received a significant amount of intellectual stimulation from Mr. Kent Aldershof of Management Strategies Incorporated, Mr. James Miller of General Tire and Rubber Company, and Dr. Jason Salsbury of American Cyanamid with respect to the initial development of our material. Our gratitude is also extended to Ms. Nancy Elliott for the many months of careful work she devoted to this project. Finally, of course, we must thank our families for their never ending patience.

Note

1. Alfred P. Sloan, *My Years with General Motors* (Garden City, N.Y.: Doubleday, 1964), p. 140.

1

Understanding and Setting the Target ROI

ROI as an Operating Concept

Investors and many managers are interested in some version of return on investment—specifically, the return they achieve on the investment they make or are held responsible for. The principal purpose of this chapter is to show how a target return on investment (ROI) suitable for operating managers depends on overall corporate goals and constraints. Later chapters concentrate on the achievement of this target ROI, given the cost-volume-profit-investment relationships faced by the operating manager.

Few terms have been defined and measured in more ways than ROI. Stockholders care about return on equity, operating managers about "income" and "investment" for which they are responsible. We acknowledge the diversity involved in measuring such terms as *income* and *investment*. The methods that we develop in later chapters are designed for use by operating managers, and ROI is defined accordingly. For our purposes, ROI is the ratio of operating earnings to capital employed (total operating investment). It is an operating concept.

This is a general definition, which avoids specific questions about elements to be included or excluded and the measurement of those elements. Our methods are applicable no matter how the firm defines and measures ROI. Specific questions about the elements to be included and excluded—such as whether plant is stated gross or net, whether or not current liabilities are included in determining investment, and so on—are treated in later chapters. In general, however, we would exclude interest on long-term debt and income taxes in calculating operating income and long-term debt in calculating investment. Thus, a general definition of ROI is

$$\text{ROI} = K = \frac{\text{operating income}}{\text{total operating assets}},$$

where measurement of operating income, for our purposes, is similar to the classical concept of earnings before interest and taxes (EBIT).

1

The Interdependence of ROI and Corporate Objectives

The major premise of this chapter is that top management sets an ROI target to guide decision making and performance appraisal. Further, corporate management establishes the target in conjunction with other corporate goals and constraints. In other words, the target is normally the result of prior analysis. It is a target because its achievement promotes the achievement of overall goals. We do not consider the important behavioral questions of whether or not operating managers accept the goal or participate in setting it. Our concern is principally with the relationships of corporate goals and constraints to the target operating ROI. This section will illustrate how an ROI target may be set; how it depends on other objectives; how it may or must be changed; and how tradeoffs in other corporate goals can be analyzed when ROI is a given and management changes another goal or when some constraint, such as the income-tax rate, is changed.

At least at the corporate level, a target ROI is dependent on or correlated with other important targets or operating constraints. At a minimum, these other important factors must be considered:

1. *Target rate of return on stockholder equity (ROE):* A satisfactory value for this ratio—net income divided by stockholder equity—is one of the principal goals of corporations. Preferred stock is ignored for the sake of simplicity, but it could easily be included if ROE is defined as earnings available for common equity (net income minus dividends on preferred stock divided by common equity). ROE is one of the measures of financial success most frequently mentioned in the literature, in annual reports, and in the financial press.

2. *Target growth in earnings:* This goal is inherent in any planning environment and is typically stated as the target compound annual growth in net income (earnings after interest and taxes).

3. *Target dividend payout ratio:* Although statements of corporate dividend policy take many forms, the most common is the payout ratio, measured as the proportion of earnings after interest and taxes paid to stockholders. We will assume that the firm sets a specific payout ratio, or earnings retention ratio, as part of its planning process. A constant payout ratio gives dividends the same growth rate as earnings.

4. *Target debt ratio:* Objectives relative to the firm's desired capital structure are most often stated as target debt ratios, the proportion of total assets financed by debt. The calculation of this ratio generally involves total debt divided by total assets (both short- and long-term debt). This is appropriate when all assets are under the control of operating managers and all liabilities under corporate control; operating managers are responsible for returns on total assets. (Appendix 1B shows the modifications needed when operating managers do not control all assets and do control some

liabilities.) In general, the debt ratio is as much a constraint as a target because external parties greatly influence it.

5. *Average cost of debt:* The cost of debt financing operates as a constraint rather than as a target and is measured by the average pretax interest rate.

6. *Corporate income-tax rate:* The average tax rate on corporate income also must be measured and incorporated in the setting of a target ROI.

These targets and constraints should be taken into account in setting a target ROI because they are all interdependent. When targets are set for earnings growth, payout ratio, and debt ratio, given specific costs of debt and tax rates, there is only one ROI that will achieve them. Moreover, the competing nature of corporate goals makes an interdependent analysis all the more important.

Of course, once corporate management sets an ROI target as a function of other objectives, it might assign different ROI targets to different divisions based on their relative abilities to contribute to the overall goal. The interaction of division managers and corporate managers in setting ROI targets would be greatly facilitated by an interdependent framework that takes into account as many goals as possible.

ROI as a Target of Corporate Objectives

The target ROI, perhaps more appropriately termed the required overall corporate ROI, may be estimated by using the following relationship.

$$K = \frac{G(1 - D)}{E(1 + G)(1 - T)} + iD,$$

where $K =$ the desired target return, before interest and taxes, on total investment, stated as of the end of the reporting period. (Managers who prefer to use beginning balances should divide the target ROI given by the foregoing formula by the quantity $(1 + G)$. We prefer to work with ending investment because the methods to be presented in the following chapters permit the evaluation of the consequences of decisions that *change* investment; such evaluations require the use of ending balances—those determined *after* the action.)

$E =$ the desired earnings retention ratio. (Stated as one minus the payout ratio. The model therefore assumes no external equity financing. We will relax this assumption shortly.)

G = the target compound annual growth in net profit (earnings after interest and taxes).

D = the target ratio of debt to total assets (measured at the end of the reporting period).

i = the average pretax cost of debt (average interest rate).

T = the corporate income-tax rate.

The target return on equity (ROE) does not appear in this formulation. Appendix 1A shows that it is redundant to use both a target growth rate in earnings and a target ROE. Although we could use either the target ROE or the target growth rate, we selected the latter because it gives a dynamic rather than a static result. The return on equity implied by the foregoing formula is:

$$\text{ROE} = \frac{G}{E(1 + G)}.$$

Whether we call these factors objectives, goals, or constraints is unimportant. What is important is that they must be considered in developing a target ROI that is based on operations, not on a combination of operations, taxation, and financing. *Financing* here means both the debt ratio and the earnings retention ratio. There are several reasons for the importance of determining a target ROI based on "pure" operating results.

First, general managers with ROI responsibility must have targets that lie within their areas of control. Corporate objectives such as the debt ratio and the growth rate in after-tax earnings are not within their control; thus, they cannot be held responsible for meeting them, even though their efforts will bear heavily on whether the firm does meet them. Their responsibilities typically relate to pretax, preinterest profits and operating assets, with no allowance for methods of financing.

Second, it is at best awkward and at worst virtually impossible to use anything but relatively pure operating results in planning and controlling operations. Trying to incorporate directly the effects of taxes, debt ratio, retention ratio, and so on in decisions involving pricing, output, credit terms, and investment (to name some of those to be considered in subsequent chapters) is neither feasible nor desirable. Operating managers, as well as marketing managers and financial managers at the divisional level, have enough to think about without these added burdens.

The model presented here is obviously not the only possible one. However, corporate management must have some way of translating overall goals and constraints into a statement of target operating results; this model is straightforward and comprehensive enough for this purpose.

The initial implications of this planning model may be observed by analyzing table 1-1, where the required target ROI is stated as a function of various values of desired or expected earnings growth, G, earnings retention ratio, E, and debt ratio, D. The table assumes an average interest rate of ten percent and an average corporate income tax rate of 46 percent.

Several important relationships between the target ROI and other goals and constraints can be observed in table 1-1. First, the target ROI is a linear function of the debt ratio, D. In general, the target ROI decreases linearly with an increase in the target debt ratio. (The exception for the figures in table 1-1 can be found where $E = 100$ percent and $G = 5$ percent). Moreover, the higher the target growth rate in earnings, the greater the benefit (in the form of a reduced target ROI) of an increase in the debt

Table 1-1
Determining the Return-on-Investment Target

(D) Target Debt Ratio (Percent)	(E) Target Earnings Retention Ratio (Percent)	(G) Target Earnings Growth (Percent)						
		5	10	15	20	25	30	35
0	100	8.8	16.8	24.2	30.9	37.0	42.7	48.0
	80	11.0	21.0	30.2	38.6	46.3	53.4	60.0
	60	14.7	28.1	40.3	51.4	61.7	71.2	80.0
	40	22.0	42.1	60.4	77.2	92.6	106.8	120.0
	20	44.1	84.2	120.8	154.3	185.2	213.7	240.1
20	100	9.1	15.5	21.3	26.7	31.6	36.2	40.4
	80	10.8	18.8	26.2	32.9	39.0	44.7	50.0
	60	13.8	24.4	34.2	43.2	51.4	59.0	66.0
	40	19.6	35.7	48.3	63.7	76.1	87.5	98.0
	20	37.3	69.3	96.6	125.5	150.1	172.9	194.0
40	100	9.3	14.1	18.5	22.5	26.2	29.6	32.8
	80	10.6	16.6	22.1	27.1	31.8	36.1	40.0
	60	12.8	20.8	28.2	34.9	41.0	46.7	52.0
	40	17.2	29.3	40.2	50.3	59.6	68.1	76.0
	20	30.5	54.5	76.5	96.6	115.1	132.2	148.0
60	100	9.5	12.7	15.7	18.3	20.8	23.1	25.2
	80	10.4	14.4	18.1	21.4	24.5	27.4	30.0
	60	11.9	17.2	22.1	26.6	30.7	34.5	38.0
	40	14.8	22.8	30.2	36.9	43.0	48.7	54.0
	20	23.6	39.7	54.3	67.7	80.1	91.5	102.0
80	100	9.8	11.4	12.8	14.2	15.4	16.5	17.6
	80	10.2	12.2	14.0	15.7	17.3	18.7	20.0
	60	10.9	13.6	16.1	18.3	20.3	22.2	24.0
	40	12.4	16.4	20.1	23.4	26.5	29.4	32.0
	20	16.8	24.8	32.2	38.9	45.0	50.7	56.0

Note: Average interest rate (i) = 10 percent, income-tax rate (T) = 46 percent.

ratio. If we define ΔK as the required change in the target ROI given a change equal to ΔD in the target debt ratio, then the relation is

$$\Delta K = \left[i - \frac{G}{E(1 + G)(1 - T)} \right] \Delta D$$

Thus, as long as $G/[E(1 + G)(1 - T)]$ is greater than i, the target ROI decreases linearly with an increase in the target debt ratio. This relationship assumes, of course, that the average interest rate on debt, i, is unrelated to the debt ratio—an unlikely possibility over a wide range of debt ratios, but perfectly plausible over fairly narrow ranges. Rarely would managers contemplate extremely large changes in the debt ratio. The required change in the target ROI, given a change in the average interest rate, is simply

$$\Delta K = D\Delta i.$$

Second, as a firm reduces its target earnings retention ratio – meaning that it plans to increase its payout ratio—the required change in the target ROI rises rapidly. Additionally, the impact is greatest at higher target growth rates. It is true that, for a given EBIT, a higher payout ratio implies a higher ROI; but the target return grows substantially. The relationship between a change in the target earnings retention ratio and a change in the required target ROI is further illustrated in figure 1-1.

Third, as a firm increases its target annual earnings growth, the re-

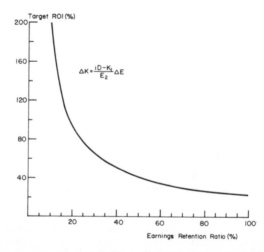

Figure 1-1. Target ROI and Earnings Retention Ratio

quired target ROI increases, but at a decreasing rate. This can be seen in figure 1-2. However, the fact that the target ROI increases at a decreasing rate with increases in the growth target is primarily academic. As figure 1-2 clearly demonstrates, substantial ROIs are necessary to sustain reasonable rates of growth.

Finally, a change in the income-tax rate, other things being equal, can have a significant effect on the target ROI. This relationship is illustrated in figure 1-3. As we demonstrate in subsequent chapters, a change in the target ROI can have a significant impact on prices, output, and the level of investment. Thus, a change in the income-tax rate will also have a significant effect on the required levels of prices, output, and investment by altering the firm's target return on investment.

ROI as the Precursor of Corporate Objectives

Our previous discussion viewed the setting of a target ROI as, one might say, the dependent variable governed by corporate goals. It is certainly important for an operating manager to understand ROI in this framework, in order to comprehend more clearly the pressures on corporate managers and the attendant setting of the target ROI. However, the setting of operating objectives is not nearly so flexible. (No human interactions are). Operating units do business in industries or markets that might sharply limit their degrees of freedom and place rather tight bands around ROI possibilities. At this writing, we are confident that if corporate managers in the tire and rubber industry desired growth (G) of 12 percent, an earnings retention ratio (E) of 60 percent, and a debt ratio (D) of 40 percent, their tire divisions would be hard pressed to contribute one-half of the 28.2-percent ROI implied by table 1-1. Since the tire divisions of these firms make up a huge proportion of corporate results, such a set of corporate objectives is simply not possible over any reasonable planning horizon. At the other end of the spectrum, some firms in the semiconductor industry are showing incredible rates of earnings growth coupled with no need for external financing precisely because their operating divisions are generating tremendous ROIs.

Thus, at times we must view ROI as an independent variable, a given, in the setting of corporate objectives. More specifically, we might say that the results derived from operations (K) underlie corporate profitability (ROE) and growth (G), whereas decisions regarding capital structure (D and E) serve either to enhance or hinder the effects of operations.

In order to develop this view, we rearrange the target-ROI relation into a growth relation.

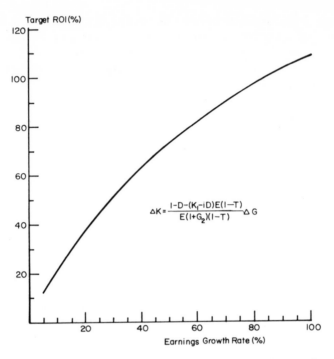

Figure 1–2. Target ROI and Target Growth in Earnings

$$G = \frac{E(K - iD)(1 - T)}{1 - D - E(K - iD)(1 - T)}.$$

In this relation, after-tax earnings as a proportion of ending total assets is defined by $(K - iD)(1 - T)$, which is the after-tax, after-interest return on total investment. Thus, $E(K - iD)(1 - T)$ is the proportion of net income reinvested in the firm. The debt ratio then provides a multiplier effect in supporting the growth potential of these reinvested earnings. Table 1–2 outlines this relation and dramatically illustrates the growth-supporting potential of ROI and how this potential may be enhanced by capital structure decisions. Whether or not the markets the firm serves can support these growth rates over the planning horizon is obviously another question. The critical question is not whether, say, the total market is growing at the rate G, but whether the firm can find opportunities to invest at the target ROI that are sufficient to yield the target growth rate.

The model shows extremely high growth rates, which of course are not indefinitely sustainable. Over the planning horizons of most corporations,

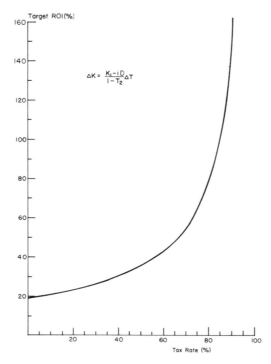

Figure 1-3. Target ROI and the Income-Tax Rate

however, many of these growth rates are quite conceivable. Even some of the growth rates that may be considered "pathological" have been observed. One need only recall how some firms in the computer-leasing industry employed new equity issues and high debt ratios to maintain enormous rates of growth while earning only about a 10-percent ROE. Their world eventually came crashing down, but a large number of investors were deceived for quite some time.[1]

Table 1-2 illustrates the roles of ROI and capital structure in several important ways. First, note that although return on equity (ROE) was previously defined as a function of growth (G) and earnings retention (E), it may also be defined in terms of ROI and the debt ratio. As many readers are already aware, the *static* definition of ROE is

$$\text{ROE} = \frac{(K - iD)(1 - T)}{1 - D},$$

which simply states that return on equity is defined by the after-tax return

Table 1-2
Potential Rates of Earnings Growth
(percent)

D	E		K						
		15	*20*	*25*	*30*	*35*	*40*	*45*	*50*
	50	3.9	5.3	6.7	8.1	9.6	11.1	12.7	14.3
	75	6.0	8.1	10.3	12.7	15.1	17.6	20.3	23.1
0	100	8.1	11.1	14.3	17.6	21.2	25.0	29.0	33.3
	125	10.3	14.3	18.5	23.1	28.0	33.3	39.1	45.5
	150	12.7	17.6	23.1	29.0	35.6	42.9	50.9	60.0
	ROE	7.5	10.0	12.5	15.0	17.5	20.0	22.5	25.0
	50	4.3	6.2	8.1	10.1	12.1	14.3	16.5	18.8
	75	6.7	9.6	12.7	15.9	19.4	23.1	27.0	31.1
25	100	9.1	13.2	17.6	22.4	27.7	33.3	39.5	46.3
	125	11.6	17.1	23.1	29.7	37.1	45.5	54.8	65.5
	150	14.3	21.2	29.0	37.9	48.1	60.0	73.9	90.5
	ROE	8.3	11.7	15.0	18.3	21.7	25.0	28.3	31.7
	50	5.3	8.1	11.1	14.3	17.6	21.2	25.0	29.0
	75	8.1	12.7	17.6	23.1	29.0	35.6	42.9	50.9
50	100	11.1	17.6	25.0	33.3	42.9	53.8	66.7	81.8
	125	14.3	23.1	33.3	45.5	60.0	77.8	100.0	128.6
	150	17.6	29.0	42.9	60.0	81.8	110.5	150.0	207.7
	ROE	10.0	15.0	20.0	25.0	30.0	35.0	40.0	45.0
	50	8.1	14.3	21.2	29.0	37.9	48.1	60.0	73.9
	75	12.7	23.1	35.6	50.9	70.2	95.1	128.6	175.9
75	100	17.6	33.3	53.8	81.8	122.2	185.7	300.0	566.7
	125	23.1	45.5	77.8	128.6	220.0	433.3	*	*
	150	29.0	60.0	110.5	207.7	471.4	*	*	*
	ROE	15.0	25.0	35.0	45.0	55.0	65.0	75.0	85.0

Note: i = 10 percent, T = 50 percent. Retention rates (E) greater than 100 mean equity issues. * = very large.

on investment divided by the proportion of the firm's assets financed by equity. Thus, ROI is a prime determinant of ROE.

Second, we can note from table 1-2 that operating results, as reflected by ROI, can "support" a predetermined rate of growth in earnings without any requirements for external funding. (Again, whether or not the market will support these rates is an entirely different question.) These growth rates are observable in the third row of table 1-2. Thus, a firm with no debt (D = 0) that reinvests 100 percent of its earnings (E = 1) can support a growth rate given by

$$G = \frac{K(1 - T)}{1 - K(1 - T)}.$$

The term that defines internally sustainable growth, $K(1 - T)/[1 - K(1 - T)]$, is, under some circumstances, the *internal rate of return.* Therefore, a firm with a 40-percent ROI and an income-tax rate of 50 percent can sustain a growth rate of 25 percent using internally generated funds, whereas an ROI of 60 percent could support internal growth of 43 percent. (The relationship between the internal rate of return and the target ROI for capital budgeting analysis will be presented in chapter 6.) Thus, under purely internal financing, ROI is also a prime determinant of growth.

Third, one can see from table 1-2 that, for a given ROI, capital structure decisions are quite dynamic in the manner in which they support growth. The larger the ROI, of course, the greater the degrees of freedom the firm has in its methods of financing to ensure growth. The dynamic aspects of capital structure follow because both equity and debt-financing requirements increase at a decreasing rate as a function of increases in the growth target. This is especially true for debt, as illustrated in figure 1-4. Thus, at low levels of debt even a modest increase in the growth target, for a constant ROI, requires huge increases in external financing; if the firm is already highly leveraged, however, further increases in external funding are quite small even for large increases in the growth target. (These results, of course, assume that the interest rate is unaffected by the debt ratio. Although in fact it is affected, the results are still applicable, particularly if K is significantly greater than iD. At the time of this writing, the prime rate is over 18 percent—by these models an insignificant cost of debt when ROI is 40 percent.)

The old adage that "growth firms do not pay dividends" is also reinforced by table 1-2, although we might add the word "profitable" at the beginning. For instance, suppose that a firm currently earns a 40-percent ROI but operates in a mature market with earnings-growth prospects of only, say, 5 percent annually over its planning period. If the firm's debt ratio was 25 percent (and $i = 0.1$, $T = 0.5$), then the model states that the firm could pay out 81 percent of its earnings in dividends ($E = 0.19$). But would it? Given the double taxation of dividends, coupled with the fact that the firm is generating a 25-percent ROE, we doubt it. The firm could, for example, retain 75 percent of its earnings; and, assuming that it could continue past performance and find new ventures in other markets yielding 40-percent ROIs, it could provide the stockholder with a much greater return than he could find with his double-taxed dividends. Such a reinvestment policy *could* then help to support a 23-percent growth rate (see table 1-2). Even if the earnings reinvestment lowered ROI, the degrees of freedom, in the interest of the stockholder, provided by a healthy base ROI are significant.

At this point, the questions of earnings retention and the financing of growth lead to a small but important extension of the target-ROI model.

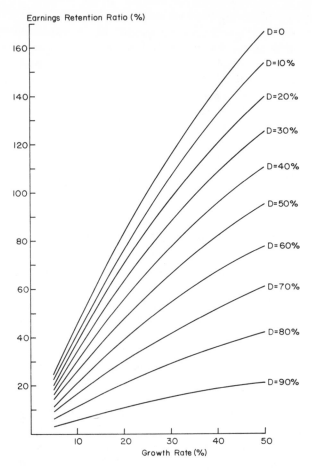

Figure 1-4. Target Growth and External Funding

We noted in the preliminary development of our approach that the model assumed no external equity financing. Although this was convenient in developing the initial relationships (see appendix 1A), it is completely unnecessary. Table 1-2 shows that values of the target earnings retention ratio (E) were allowed to exceed 100 percent. Since a firm cannot reinvest more than 100 percent of its earnings, any value greater than 100 percent simply implies external equity financing. For instance, if a firm's earnings retention ratio is 125 percent, then it must issue new equity each year equal to 25 percent of current earnings if it pays no dividends and to more than 25 percent if it does pay dividends. The target-ROI model easily allows for paying dividends and issuing new equity. If we set the target earnings retention ratio independently of other corporate goals, then we may define a new variable, Z, which represents the proportion of current earnings that the firm must raise through new equity. The relation is

$$Z = \frac{G(1 - D)}{(K - iD)(1 + G)(1 - T)} - E.$$

The value of Z might be negative, implying the purchase of treasury shares (which may be much more desirable than paying dividends). For an illustration, suppose that a firm is earning a 25-percent ROI in a market or competitive condition such that it can realistically expect earnings growth of 30 percent well into the future. The firm currently has a 75-percent retention ratio and a 50-percent debt ratio and, for a variety of reasons, does not think it is feasible to change either target. (Remember that (1) stockholders must eat, and (2) 30-percent growth means large issues of new debt just to maintain the 50-percent debt ratio.) Then, the proportion of annual earnings to be raised through new equity issues would be (with $i = 0.1$, $T = 0.5$) 40.4 percent each year over the planning horizon. On the other hand, if the ROI was 40 percent and all other values remained constant, then the value of Z would be negative (-9.1 percent)—implying that the firm could repurchase treasury shares each year in an amount equal to 9.1 percent of current earnings. Again, a healthy ROI yields great flexibility in achieving corporate objectives.

It is certainly true that if the firm is issuing or buying back stock, its growth rate (G) does not mean that earnings *per share* are growing at a rate G. Relating an earnings-growth rate to an earnings-per-share growth rate is a fairly simple matter given the price-earnings ratio. Of course, changes in that ratio would affect the relationship, as would any other changes. Moreover, the price-earnings ratio will reflect the growth of earnings per share more than that of total earnings. If we define M as the price-earnings multiple and G' as the growth in earnings per share, then

$$G' = (1 - Z/M)G - Z/M.$$

In the preceding illustration, if the price-earnings ratio (M) was equal to 10, then the 30-percent earnings growth would yield an earnings-per-share growth (G') of 24.7 percent when ROI is 25 percent and the new-equity proportion (Z) is 40 percent. The multiple of ten times is low for such high growth rates. The higher the multiple, the closer the rate of growth in earnings per share to that of total earnings. That is not too bad when one observes the same conditions (that is, $K = 25$ percent, $D = 50$ percent, $E = 75$ percent) yield an earnings-growth potential of 17.6 percent with no new equity (see table 1–2). However, if ROI was 40 percent with a negative new-equity proportion of 9.1 percent, then the 30-percent earnings growth leads to a 31.2-percent growth in earnings per share. (It is difficult to speculate on how long repurchasing could persist. Teledyne, for example, has purchased significant amounts of treasury stock over the past several years).

As a final note on change relations, we must point out the effects of rates of interest and taxes. Figure 1–3 outlined the effect of taxes on the target ROI; and one can observe that, at current rates of corporate income taxes, increases in tax rates would place enormous pressure on the target ROI if corporate objectives remain unchanged (and, as later chapters show, would also place enormous pressure on product prices). To the extent that corporate objectives are modified with changes in rates of interest or taxes, while the target ROI remains unchanged, the outcomes of pressures are not too desirable. When interest rates or income-tax rates increase, either (1) the target growth rate must decrease; or (2) the debt ratio must increase (even with an increase in interest rates), or earnings retention must increase, or both. Neither response is destined to enhance equity values. Therefore, there must still be pressure on the target ROI.

ROI *Must* Be a Target

Whether one analyzes the return on investment as a dependent variable or an independent variable is really immaterial. The fact is that ROI *is* a target that operating managers seek to achieve. There is doubtless a certain bounded rationality in the setting of this target, but it is still a target. The target-ROI model links the goals of operating managers to corporate objectives and strategies by providing a rational, analytical basis for determining the performance criteria used for evaluating operating results. Achieving the ROI goal is a critical element of success; the rest of this book presents analytical methods for understanding the relationships among ROI and various factors—both those that operating managers control and those that constrain them.

Obviously, this chapter only scratches the surface of a complex and continually changing set of variables. Social and psychological conditions and quantifiable economic forces differ among firms; managers have (or create) different degrees of freedom in dealing with them. Nevertheless, the relations presented in this chapter are useful in analyzing corporate and operating objectives and in understanding the interactions among the various factors. It is critically important that managers understand these interactions and the implications for a change in one (say, ROI) as a function of a change in another (say, the target growth rate).

Summary

The primary emphasis of this book will be to present methods that managers can use to set prices, output, and levels of investment using the firm's target ROI as a control criterion. This chapter has dealt with establishing a target ROI and analyzing the interrelationships of a target ROI and other corporate goals and constraints.

Return on investment, ROI, was defined as earnings before interest and taxes, EBIT, divided by capital employed at the end of the reporting period. We noted how a firm's target ROI should, or must, be set in conjunction with at least three other corporate objectives: (1) the target earnings growth, measured by the compound annual growth rate in reported earnings after interest and taxes; (2) the target earnings retention ratio, measured by the proportion of earnings after interest and taxes retained and reinvested; and (3) the target debt ratio, measured by the proportion of total assets financed by debt. In addition, the average cost of debt and the income-tax rate were shown to be important determinants of the target ROI.

Certainly, a business organization has many objectives beyond those articulated and illustrated in this chapter. These targets are influenced by many forces, such as the operating strategies of principal competitors, the availability of resources, the cost of equity, market conditions, and regulatory requirements. Nevertheless, the model outlined in this chapter is helpful for understanding, integrating, and monitoring interdependent corporate goals and is valuable in the overall strategic-planning process.

Note

1. W.E. Fruhan, *Financial Strategy: Studies in the Creation, Transfer, and Destruction of Stockholder Value,* chapter 7, pp. 180–208 (Homewood, Ill.: Richard D. Irwin, 1979).

Appendix 1A
Derivation of the
Target-ROI Equation

This appendix shows the derivation of the basic target-ROI formula and shows why neither total assets nor the target return on equity appear in it.

Let I_t = total assets at the *end* of year t and K' = return on end-of-year stockholder equity (net income/stockholder equity).

$$\text{ROE} = K' = \frac{(KI_t - iDI_t)(1 - T)}{I_t(1 - D)}$$

$$K' = \frac{I_t(K - iD)(1 - T)}{I_t(1 - D)}$$

$$K' = \frac{(K - iD)(1 - T)}{1 - D}.$$

The growth rate in earnings, G, is given by

$$G = \frac{I_t(K - iD)(1 - T)}{I_{t-1}(K - iD)(1 - T)} - 1,$$

$$G = \frac{I_t}{I_{t-1}} - 1.$$

In other words, the growth rate in net income equals the growth rate of total assets.

Total assets at the end of year t are equal to total assets at the end of year $(t - 1)$ plus the increase in retained earnings from operations in year t plus the increase in debt necessary to keep the target debt ratio.

Net income may be stated as $K'I_t(1 - D)$.

$$I_t = I_{t-1} + \frac{EK'I_t(1 - D)}{1 - D}$$

$$I_t = I_{t-1} + EK'I_t$$

$$I_t = \frac{I_{t-1}}{(1 - EK')}$$

Then the growth rate, G, is

$$G = \frac{I_{t-1}/(1 - EK')}{I_{t-1}} - 1$$

$$G = \frac{1}{1 - EK'} - 1 = \frac{EK'}{1 - EK'}$$

and

$$K' = \frac{G}{E(1 + G)}$$

Substituting this expression for K',

$$\frac{G}{E(1 + G)} = \frac{(K - iD)(1 - T)}{1 - D}$$

$$\frac{G(1 - D)}{E(1 + G)} = K - iD - KT + iDT$$

$$KT - K = iDT - iD - \frac{G(1 - D)}{E(1 + G)}$$

Multiplying through by -1 and rearranging,

$$K(1 - T) = iD(1 - T) + \frac{G(1 - D)}{E(1 - G)}$$

$$K = \frac{G(1 - D)}{E(1 + G)(1 - T)} + iD$$

Thus ROE (K') and investment (I) are not necessary, although some might wish to use a target ROE to determine the required retention ratio. In other words, we could use ROE as one of the variables, in which case the target growth rate and retention ratio become redundant.

Appendix 1B
Definitions of
Investment

Chapter 1 discussed ROI targets set as returns on total assets. Some firms hold operating managers responsible for return on assets, others for return on assets less some current liabilities. The current liabilities that might be included would be those associated with the operations of the unit, like trade payables and accruals. Current liabilities under the control of the corporation, like bank credit and accrued income taxes, would usually be excluded in determining the investment of an operating unit. The other side of the coin is that some corporate assets are not usually under the control of operating units, and the operating managers are not responsible for earning returns on them. Some examples are investments in securities, excess of purchase price over fair value of assets of a subsidiary (goodwill), and bond-issue costs.

This appendix shows how to calculate a target ROI based on the investment for which the individual operating units are responsible, when that investment excludes some assets and includes some liabilities. A numerical example might be helpful. Assume the following data for an illustrative firm.

Total assets (millions)	$80.0
Total liabilities (millions)	30.0
Stockholder equity (millions)	$50.0
EBIT (millions)	31.1
Interest expense and unallocated corporate expenses, net of "other income" (millions)	3.0
Tax rate (percent)	46.0
Net income (millions)	$15.2

The $3.0-million interest and unallocated corporate expenses (for example, amortization of intangible assets, some research and development) is the total of nonoperating items not allocated to divisions, net of income on assets not under divisional control (for example, investments). We now reinterpret i to mean the ratio of net unallocated corporate expenses to total debt, instead of just the rate of interest. We could continue to use *i* to denote only the interest rate and add a new term to denote other unallocated corporate expenses, but there is no reason to do so.

ROI, defined as EBIT divided by total assets, is 38.8 percent ($31.1/$80.0), which would support a growth rate of 10 percent, given a retention ratio of 30 percent, an "interest" rate of 10 percent, a tax rate of 46 percent, and a debt ratio of 37.5 percent, all of which conform to the foregoing data.

Suppose now that the operating managers are responsible for 90 percent of the total assets and 20 percent of total liabilities. The target ROI of 38.8 percent on *total assets* was given by the following formula from chapter 1.

$$K = \frac{G(1 - D)}{E(1 + G)(1 - T)} + iD.$$

That calculation does not give the operating managers their target ROI because they are not responsible for the $80-million total assets but only for $66 million: 90 percent of $80 million less 20 percent of $30-million liabilities. The ROI that they need to show, therefore is, 47.1 percent; which represents the $31.1 million divided by $66 million. The following formula gives the required ROI when operating managers are not responsible for total assets.

$$K = \frac{G(1 - D)}{E(1 + G)(1 - T)(A - LD)} + \frac{iD}{(A - LD)}.$$

where A = the percentage of total assets controlled by operating managers (90 percent here), and L = the percentage of total liabilities credited to operating managers in determining their investments (20 percent here). Using our data, K = 47.1 percent.

This formulation is appropriate whenever operating managers either do not control all assets or are credited with some liabilities. The original 38.8-percent target ROI would not do if it were calculated using the net operating investment of $66 million. In general, the target ROI will rise (in relation to the original formulation based on return on total assets) if there are assets not controlled by operating managers and if operating managers are credited with liabilities. Again, we do not take a position on whether or not the firm *should* include or exclude current liabilities or allocate corporate assets to operating units. The method shown here is general, and readers may apply it no matter how they determine the investment that they use in evaluating operating managers.

2 Measuring the Components of ROI

Chapter 1 defined ROI as operating income divided by investment, where investment was defined as capital employed by an operating unit and operating income was defined as earnings before interest and taxes (EBIT). Using these definitions (or any others, for that matter) to guide decisions regarding price, output, credit terms, inventory policy, and other variables necessitates an approach that permits the *simultaneous* estimation of operating income and investment (especially investment in current assets).

Approaches that concentrate on profit, like cost-volume-profit (CVP) analysis and markup pricing, ignore investment. Classical approaches to ROI, such as the "margin-times-turnover" model, or richer versions like the DuPont model, fail to consider the interdependencies among revenue, unit volume, and investment in current assets. Moreover, although the Du-Pont model, among others, has obvious value for *diagnostic* purposes, it provides no *analytical* guidance for planning and decision making because it does not link the critical components of profit and investment. That is, the manager must make assumptions about investment independently of his analysis of cost-volume-profit relationships. But because cost-volume-profit relationships are important determinants of investment in current assets, the manager must go through iterative trial-and-error estimates to reach a satisfactory conclusion.

The principal purpose of this chapter is to develop an approach that does allow the simultaneous estimation of income and investment and that permits the manager to evaluate the effects on ROI of changes in critical variables. We begin with the classic case of the single-product manufacturing firm, division, plant, or other operating unit. This assumption is neither restrictive nor unrealistic. The stated objectives of this book are to aid in developing applications of target-ROI methods to pricing, analyzing volume requirements, and guiding investment; because these topics essentially imply single-product analysis, such a restriction is actually desirable.

The basic analysis also holds for multiproduct operating units under several sets of circumstances. The analysis applies if managers can assign costs and investment to specific products in a reasonable fashion. It also applies if averaging across products is reasonable. For instance, if product mix is relatively stable, then it is appropriate to speak of an "average" unit of product. Subsequent chapters will discuss how this restriction may be either relaxed or handled effectively.

Most readers probably will use book-value figures in applying the model. However, the model is general and accommodates replacement-cost data or price-level-adjusted data as well as book values. However, the use of book values follows the basic definition of ROI most often employed in practice, especially for performance evaluation. Additionally, the use of book values introduces no requirements for information gathering and measurement not already available from a typical firm's accounting system. Of course, the Securities and Exchange Commission (SEC) and the Financial Accounting Standards Board (FASB) have been moving toward alternative valuation bases; we might expect greater use of these. If the information is then routinely collected to meet reporting requirements, it will probably find more use for managerial purposes. Interested readers might wish to verify for themselves through experimentation that the approach easily accommodates replacement-cost or price-level-adjusted data.

Estimating the Components of Operating Profit (EBIT)

The most commonly used model for profit planning and analysis is the method of cost-volume-profit (CVP) analysis, which is typically stated as

$$\text{EBIT} = \text{Volume (Price } - \text{ Variable Cost)} - \text{Fixed Costs}$$
$$= Q(P - V) - F.$$

For a variety of reasons, this is an inappropriate model for analyzing return on investment. The most obvious problem is that ROI depends on investment as well as on profit, but this model says nothing about investment. The next-most-important problem is the lack of separation of cost components into those costs that are inventoried and those that are not. In addition, particularly where pricing considerations are concerned, *variable cost* is too vague a term. Costs vary in many ways, some with revenue, some with unit volume. Some variable costs are inventoried and therefore affect investment; others are not. Thus, we express EBIT as

$$\text{EBIT} = QP(1 - S) - QU - QV - F - F' - dI.$$

A fairly detailed outline of each component follows.

Q = unit sales volume. This value encompasses actual sales volume for analysis purposes, budgeted sales volume for planning purposes, and production volume. We deal with an equilibrium situation, where production equals sales, in order to avoid the sticky question of income determination under absorption costing. We do assume absorption costing for inventory determination. If we relax the assumption of sales equaling production, then we must introduce a term to deal with the inventory effect on income. We recognize that the assumption that sales equals production causes problems in the examination of changes in volume for their effects on ROI. But except in extreme cases, involving huge increases or decreases in inventory and very high fixed costs, there should be no serious problem. (Appendix 2A treats the general problems of analyzing income and investment under historical cost accounting.)

P = unit selling price. A significant portion of this book is devoted to the determination of a target unit selling price. For the time being, however, it is important only to note that P represents the gross unit selling price, that is, the quoted price to the customer before any discounts for prompt payment or for high-volume purchases. (Chapter 4 describes the use of prompt-payment discounts.)

S = selling expenses that vary with sales dollars, not necessarily with unit sales. S is stated as a percentage. In order to explore the effects of changing selling prices in some later analyses, we must include this type of cost. An obvious example of this component is commissions paid on the basis of revenue. A management fee based on dollar volume that is levied by corporate headquarters on divisions also fits into this category. Thus, this component includes any element of cost that, by policy or otherwise, typically varies with revenue rather than strictly with unit volume. For accounting purposes, the costs represented by the product QPS are charged to selling, general, and administrative expenses (that is, they are not inventoried).

U = selling expenses that vary with unit volume. Examples of such costs are packaging and shipping, commissions paid on a per-unit basis, and other distribution costs. The distinction between S and U is a matter both of policy and of good recordkeeping and analysis. Again, the costs represented by the product QU are charged to selling, general, and administrative expenses.

V = variable manufacturing costs. This component includes all variable costs of production. It is sometimes necessary, however, to expand this component into, first, the cost of raw materials and purchased components and, second, "all other" variable production costs (essentially, direct labor and variable manufacturing overhead). Thus, we shall occasionally employ the notation $V = V' + R$, where R represents the per-unit cost of raw materials and purchased components and V' represents all other unit variable production costs. For accounting purposes, these costs become part of inventory and ultimately part of cost of goods sold.

F = fixed manufacturing costs requiring cash outlays. Any manufacturing cost, exclusive of depreciation, that does not vary in the short run as a function of unit volume would be included in this component. The experienced reader is, of course, aware of the difficulties involved in separating manufacturing overhead into its fixed and variable components. This issue will not be dealt with here. It suffices to say that such a separation requires some significant effort. Thus, we simply assume that analysts have estimated the fixed and variable components of costs like supplies, utilities, and indirect labor. These costs are inventoried.

F = fixed selling, general, and administrative expenses requiring cash outlays. Some difficulty in separating fixed and variable selling expenses exists here, as it does in the manufacturing sector (in general, the problem is the same). However, a question may arise with respect to how these costs are budgeted, as opposed to how they are incurred. For instance, if a firm budgets for advertising as a percentage of sales, one would be tempted to consider this a component of S rather than of F'. However, this is rarely how advertising is actually *spent*. Therefore, it is up to the user of these methods to decide how to treat these items. For accounting purposes, F' is not inventoried.

I = book value of property, plant, and equipment, to be reported at the end of the accounting period. As noted earlier, ROI is typically a book concept. Certainly, for EBIT determination, depreciation is ordinarily based on historical cost. Readers who would rather work with an implicit EBIT concept in which investment and depreciation are measured by, for example, replacement costs, will find no difficulty.

d = current depreciation rate on book investment. Firms define d so that dI equals total depreciation for the planning period, regardless of the depreciation method used. Because dI equals total depreciation, we could simply use one letter to denote total depreciation, rather than multiplying a rate by total fixed assets. The reason for using the rate and the dollar investment will become clear in chapter 6. For accounting purposes, depreciation on assets used in manufacturing is part of production cost and is inventoried. We define m as the proportion of fixed investment allocated to manufacturing, so that depreciation equal to mdI would be inventoried and eventually would flow through to cost of goods sold, whereas depreciation equal to $(1 - m)dI$ would be charged to selling, general, and administrative expenses.

This model of earnings before interest and taxes is sufficiently comprehensive to represent a manufacturing firm, division, or other operating unit that meets the basic assumption of an essentially single-product organization. Readers who find that one or more terms are irrelevant to their operations can drop them when experimenting with the model. For example, the term QPS disappears if all variable selling costs vary with unit volume rather than directly with dollar volume. We have included as many types of cost as we think a manager is likely to have to consider, in order to provide as complete a picture as possible.

Estimating the Components of Investment

The remaining task is to relate the components of EBIT to total investment. The fixed portion of total investment (property, plant, and equipment) is generally no problem. Managers know, or can estimate very closely, the book value (or other value, such as replacement cost) of fixed assets when they plan for the short term. Therefore, current assets require most of our attention.

The way to relate specific current assets to revenue and cost components is through turnovers. Managers in many firms will find fairly stable turnovers of individual current-asset items based on either historical results or decisions regarding credit terms, desired cash balances, and inventory policy. Moreover, for planning purposes—including the budgeting of current assets—analyzing and estimating turnovers is essential.

Turnovers, and therefore investment in current assets, are to some extent within the control of the manager; but attempts to improve them might have undesirable effects because they interact with other key variables such as volume and price. A firm could reduce receivables to zero (turnover = infinity) by refusing to sell on credit; but volume would almost certainly decline, perhaps drastically. (The whole range of decisions involving tradeoffs among turnovers, volume, price, and other critical variables occupies a great deal of chapters 4 and 5.) We define the turnover of any current asset as some measure of activity for that asset divided by its ending balance. Many managers use averages to compute turnovers. As long as turnovers are reasonably stable, we can state them either way. Using year-end balance sheet data does provide simplicity; but, more importantly, we use the ending balance because we will be concerned with how much investment the firm will have *after* it achieves specific operating results or after it makes changes in operations that would change investment. Thus,

$$\text{Turnover} = \frac{\text{Measure of activity}}{\text{Ending balance}} \text{, and}$$

$$\text{Ending balance} = \frac{\text{Measure of activity}}{\text{Turnover}},$$

since we assume turnover is known (or estimated).

The critical components of current assets for ROI analysis are usually cash and equivalents (although at the operating level cash equivalents are likely to be negligible), accounts receivable, raw materials inventory, and in-process and finished goods inventory. Using the method outlined previously for estimating an asset value, we can include or exclude any of these four components with no conceptual or computational difficulty. For instance, if a division keeps little or no cash (that is, if corporate headquarters handles all significant disbursements), and if the divisional manager is not held responsible for allocated cash, then the cash term may simply be eliminated.

We now discuss each component of current assets and its relationship to revenue and cost items.

Cash

The most appropriate measure of activity for estimating cash balances is usually total cash disbursements for the period. In the context of EBIT components, total cash disbursements may reasonably be estimated as

$$\text{Total cash disbursements} = QPS + QU + QV + F + F'.$$

Suppose that the firm's policy is to keep one month's disbursements of cash on hand. Then cash turnover would be twelve times. If additional compensating balances are required by the firm's banks, then turnover might be somewhat lower. Thus, we can denote the ending cash balance by

$$\text{Ending cash balance} = \frac{QPS + QU + QV + F + F'}{t_c},$$

where t_c represents cash turnover.

Some managers might prefer to use sales revenue rather than total disbursements as the measure of activity for estimating cash balances, and to adjust the activity figure accordingly. For example, corporate headquarters might handle all cash disbursements but might also allocate cash to divisions based on total revenue for purposes of evaluating divisional performance. Following this approach, we could estimate cash as QP/t_c. Of course, the value of the turnover based on revenue would differ from the one based on cash disbursements. Although we have no objection to such an approach, we believe that total disbursements are more representative, particularly for divisions of larger firms.

Although we think that our formulation of cash requirements is generally about as good as possible, we expect that managers will modify it more than any of the terms. Some firms and divisions use sophisticated cash-planning models that consider both expected receipts and expected disbursements, allowing managers to spot opportunities for reducing non-interest-bearing cash. Even so, a formulation like ours will probably come close to predicting actual cash requirements. From a practical point of view, operating managers should formulate the cash term exactly as corporate headquarters charges them with cash, whether it is related to total revenue, cost of sales, or whatever.

Accounts Receivable

The measure of activity for estimating the ending balance for accounts receivable is, obviously, sales. Thus, receivables will be denoted by

$$\text{Ending accounts receivable} = QP/t_a,$$

where t_a represents accounts receivable turnover. (If the firm uses revenue to determine cash balances, then it may combine cash and receivables into a single term because they both have total revenue in the numerator.) Managers accustomed to thinking in terms of average collection period or day's sales in receivables need only divide 360 (or 365) by the collection period to obtain the turnover. If the firm's average collection period is sixty days, then t_a is 6. One of the benefits of the approach followed in this book is that it provides a framework for analyzing such policy variables as credit terms and for estimating their effects on prices, output, and ROI.

Raw Materials Inventory

The measure of activity for raw materials inventory is the total cost of raw materials and purchased components used in production. We assume that production equals sales and that the cost of raw materials purchased equals their use. The cost of raw materials used will be denoted by QR, where R represents the cost of raw materials and purchased components per unit of finished product. Obviously, this is a composite figure for products that require more than one material or component.

The turnover of raw materials is typically a question of policy. Certainly, the determination of the policy is a difficult matter. Chapters 4, 5, and 6 show how managers can evaluate changes in inventory policy that involve tradeoffs of turnovers with costs (such as the cost of installing an inventory-control system). Firms develop a policy of, for example, keeping one month's supply of raw materials and purchased components on hand. In that case, raw materials inventory turns over twelve times. Thus, this account will be denoted by

$$\text{Raw materials inventory} = QR/t_r,$$

where t_r represents the turnover of raw materials and purchased components.

The topic of inventories provides a convenient place to return to the question of definition or measurement of investment. In some firms, operating managers are held responsible for returns on assets, with no current liabilities allowed in the calculation of investment. In others, managers do get the benefit of having current liabilities included in the determination of investment. No assumption about this matter is made here. The model can be used in either case through appropriate restatements of turnovers.

For instance, if raw materials turn over 12 times a year and trade payables generally equal 25 percent of raw materials (that is, payables turn over 48 times), then a turnover of 16 would result in stating materials net of payables. Of course, this argument applies to any component of current assets and its measure of turnover. For example, accruals could be offset against cash in similar fashion.

The net turnover of an asset and related liability, one that turns over with the same measure of activity as the asset, is determined by the formula,

$$t_n = \frac{t_A t_L}{t_L - t_A},$$

where t_n = the net turnover, t_A = the turnover of the asset, and t_L = the turnover of the liability. Appendix 3B deals with the case in which the manager wants to state each current asset and current liability separately, not netted out. We do not need that refinement yet.

The merits of including or excluding current liabilities for evaluating divisional performance are not of concern here. We assume that the reader has decided this question (or that corporate headquarters has done so) and will determine his turnovers accordingly.

In-Process and Finished Goods Inventories

The measure of activity for these accounts is total production cost, or cost of sales, because sales equals production. Therefore, we can combine them into a single figure even though, taken separately, they probably turn over at different rates.

The formula for combining two current assets that turn over with the same measure of activity is

$$t_T = \frac{t_1 t_2}{t_1 + t_2},$$

where t_T = combined turnover, and t_1 and t_2 = the turnovers of the individual assets. Thus, if work-in-process inventory turns over 6 times based on total production cost, and finished goods turn over 12 times on the same basis, the combined turnover is only 4 times, $(6 \times 12)/18$.

Many financial analysts use sales to calculate inventory turnover, but this is inappropriate for internal analysis and performance evaluation. Moreover, the real objective here is to estimate ending inventory, which is valued at cost. We denote these inventories by

$$\text{Ending in-process and finished inventory} = \frac{QV + F + mdI}{t_i},$$

where $(QV + F + mdI)$ represents cost of sales and t_i represents the combined turnover of in-process and finished goods. We use absorption costing for inventory, which is required for financial reporting and income-tax purposes and probably dominates internal reporting as well. Firms that use variable (direct) costing (which we certainly recommend) for internal purposes may simply drop the fixed elements, so that inventory would equal QV/t_i. A retailer or wholesaler would take this approach.

We believe that the aforementioned terms capture virtually all the current assets (and, if desired, the current liabilities) that a *division* is likely to have. (The exceptions are short-term prepayments, which should be negligible, and any bank credit, which most divisions probably do not include in their ROI calculations.) Firms usually have other assets, such as investments in securities, goodwill, and various deferred charges. These could be included in fixed assets, I, because they do not vary with activity; or they could be ignored. They are not operating assets, and we think it is desirable to work with operating results. Finally, merchandising firms have only one type of inventory and would be able to use a single term to represent it.

We are now ready to relate the income-statement and balance-sheet values to one another in a comprehensive ROI model.

The Model of Return on Investment

Combining the components of EBIT with the related measures of investment yields an operational definition of ROI. This is stated as

$$\text{ROI} = K = \frac{QP(1 - S) - QU - QV - F - F' - dI}{\dfrac{QPS + QU + QV + F + F'}{t_c} + \dfrac{QP}{t_a} + \dfrac{QR}{t_r} + \dfrac{QV + F + mdI}{t_i} + I}$$

Although this operational definition of ROI is quite long, it is easy to work with for profit planning, determining target prices, analyzing volume and investment, and investigating variances in evaluating performance. It is simple to program for use at a terminal or on a programmable calculator. About the only types of cost omitted are those that vary with the level of investment, such as inventory carrying costs, which we do recognize implicitly because we require that the target ROI be earned on inventories. It also has considerable intuitive appeal from a practical standpoint, because it relies only on the common terms of CVP analysis and turnovers, requiring only information that managers can generally obtain at little cost.

Although this model seems to describe a manufacturing firm quite well, some readers will want to modify terms to fit their own situations more closely. An obvious example would be that of managers whose units use direct costing, who would drop the fixed elements from the numerator of the inventory term. Different relationships will yield different results; and, more importantly, the equations that we will use later will not usually fit if our terms are modified. A person with reasonable algebraic competence can derive the appropriate form of any equation used in this book.

This model is obviously more complicated in appearance than, for example, the margin-times-turnover or DuPont models. The question that arises is whether the increased complexity that results from the combination of elements of profit and investment in a single equation is worthwhile. We believe that it is and spend the rest of this book showing why.

Illustrative Division

Table 2–1 presents data for a division that will be used for illustrative purposes throughout the book. For brevity, we will refer to this division as HMD (hypothetical manufacturing division). We have chosen to call the illustrative operating unit a division, rather than a firm, simply because a division is a standard operating unit with ROI responsibility in most firms. The analyses would hold if the division were a firm, a business group, or any other organization unit with ROI responsibility.

It is often difficult to develop data for illustrative purposes. There is always the question of whether the particular numerical values used are likely to be representative of those that actual divisions might expect.

There is also the possibility that focusing on only one hypothetical situation will yield results that the reader considers overly dramatic and that lead him to conclude that the entire model is inappropriate. These are real dangers. One alternative is to enumerate a larger number of hypothetical situations that we consider representative of certain well-known industries. This, however, is essentially impossible within a finite number of pages. Granted, for any single variable (such as, for example, accounts receivable turnover), the variation among industry categories is typically greater than

Table 2-1
Hypothetical Manufacturing Division

S, G, and A expenses varying with revenue (S)	11%
S, G, and A expenses varying per unit (U)	$1.50
Variable manufacturing cost (V)	10.00
Raw-materials cost (R)	7.00
Fixed manufacturing cost, cash (F)	50.0 million
Fixed S, G, and A expenses, cash (F')	10.0 million
Plant and equipment (I)	160.0 million
Depreciation rate (d)	10%
Percentage of depreciation allocated to manufacturing (m)	80%
Turnovers:	
Cash (t_c)	24
Receivables (t_a)	4
Raw materials (t_r)	6
In-process and finished goods (t_i)	5

the variation within categories; but when all these variables are taken together, the variation within categories becomes enormous.

We have therefore decided to use a single HMD. This decision requires us to pay particular attention to how various effects will be modified by different magnitudes of turnovers, costs, and fixed investments, so that readers may better understand their own situations. With respect to turnovers, the values in table 2-1 are fairly representative and do not yield overly dramatic results. In this and subsequent chapters, we will illustrate carefully the sensitivity of the model to each of these turnovers. With respect to cost structure and fixed investment, we will handle a variety of situations by presenting an extremely wide range of volume (Q) for most applications of the model. This allows us simultaneously to vary the operating leverage (meaning the ratio of total fixed costs to total variable costs) of our HMD as well as the capital intensity. We will at various times be presenting results ranging from a volume of 2 million units up to one of 50 million units. Clearly, no single division would have such a wide relevant range. We interpret the results, then, as representing those we might expect from divisions with relatively high fixed costs and fixed investment (low volume) and with relatively lower fixed costs and fixed investment. The point is that the proportion of fixed costs to variable costs is often critical; therefore, we show how divisions with different operating characteristics should respond differently. Rather than change fixed and variable costs, we shall simply use a range of volume that makes the relative amounts of these costs change considerably.

Volume Requirements

One of the most common uses of CVP analysis is in finding the volume required for a particular target profit. Using the combined ROI–CVP model, we would determine the volume needed for a target ROI, K. The formula is long, but basically simple.

$$Q = \frac{F + F' + dI + K[(F + F')/t_c + (F + mdI)/t_i + I]}{P(1 - S) - U - V - K[(PS + U + V)/t_c + P/t_a + R/t_r + V/t_i]}$$

Let us examine this equation, beginning with the denominator. The denominator is nothing more than contribution margin, $P(1 - S) - U - V$, minus the target return on the portion of investment that varies with volume. Thus, each additional unit increases the need for cash balances, $(PS + U + V)/t_c$; for receivables, P/t_a; for inventories of raw materials, R/t_r; and for in-process and finished inventories, V/t_i. We multiply all by the target ROI. Thus, the denominator is the "contribution per unit," allowing for the target ROI on the components of investment that vary with volume.

The numerator consists of fixed costs plus the required return on investment that does not change with volume. Cash balances must include fixed manufacturing and $S,G\&A$ expenses, $(F + F'(/t_c$; inventories of in-process and finished goods have a fixed component, $(F + mdI)/t_i$; and the investment in plant and equipment is also fixed.

The denominator is especially important: It will appear whenever we consider volume. One of the manager's tasks is to determine what the firm must do in the face of a change in a critical variable (for example, unit variable manufacturing costs) to maintain ROI. The denominator, which we call the *volume-change coefficient,* is a critical factor in all such analyses when the manager is interested in the change in volume required to maintain ROI (or, naturally, to increase it). For our HMD, the 40-percent-ROI volume-change coefficient is $10.69 at a price of $30.00 per unit, of which $4.51 is the required return on variable investment.

ROI Graph

Figure 2–1 presents the behavior of revenue, costs, investment, and the required return on investment in graphical form, using the data supplied in table 2–1, with a $30.00 selling price. The graph shows revenue and expense,

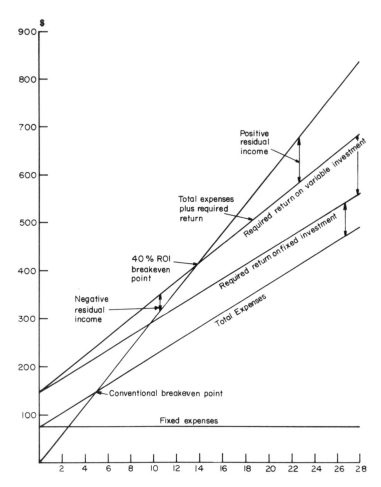

Figure 2-1. ROI Breakeven Graph

as does the familiar CVP graph. It also shows the residual income, or loss, at each volume for a target ROI of 40 percent. A target ROI of 40 percent is needed to yield, for example, an earnings-growth rate of 15 percent with a debt ratio of 40 percent, an interest rate of 10 percent, an earnings retention rate of 40 percent, and a tax rate of 46 percent. A lower target ROI would reduce the slope and intercept of the line labeled "total expenses plus required return" but would not change the basic relationships.

Residual income has its usual meaning: profit minus the target ROI multiplied by total investment. (Multiplying the target ROI by total investment gives the dollar profit needed to achieve the target ROI). The difference between the line "total expenses plus required return" and the line "total expenses" is 40 percent of total investment at the given level of volume. The figure shows the required income split between the amounts needed to cover "fixed investment" and investment that varies with volume. The split is for illustrative purposes and is not necessarily needed for analysis.

The graph shows that the HMD breaks even, in the conventional sense of a zero profit, at a volume of 5 million units, as given by the traditional breakeven equation,

$$Q = \frac{F + F' + dI}{P(1 - S) - U - V},$$

but does not earn the target ROI until it achieves a volume of 13.66 million units. The intercept of the required return lines, minus total expenses, is the income that must be earned to provide the target ROI on plant and equipment and on the components of cash and inventory that do not change with volume. Cash equal to fixed cash disbursements divided by cash turnover is the base cash required, regardless of volume. Fixed costs in inventory, both those requiring cash disbursement (F) and those requiring depreciation (mdI) also remain constant regardless of volume (again under the assumption that sales equal production). The required return on fixed investment is

$$K \left(\frac{F + F'}{t_c} + \frac{F + mdI}{t_i} + I \right).$$

The required return on investment that varies with volume is

$$K \left(\frac{PS + U + V}{t_c} + \frac{P}{t_a} + \frac{R}{t_r} + \frac{V}{t_i} \right).$$

It is worth noting that both investment and the required dollar return rise linearly with volume. Additionally, the slope of the line representing the required return is sharper than the slope of the total-expense line. As we shall see in more detail later, ignoring variable investment with increases in volume creates cash-flow problems. The slope of the line representing required return depends on several things, one of which is turnover. Other things being equal, the lower the turnover of any current asset, the greater the slope.

This form of graph seems much more informative to managers than the standard CVP graph. Managers can examine the effects on ROI of changes in volume, not just the effects on profit.

Sensitivity Analysis

At this point it is appropriate to outline the effects on ROI of changes in some components of EBIT and investment. We can begin by analyzing the effects of a change in unit volume. When a change in sales, denoted by ΔQ, occurs, the change in EBIT is

$$\Delta(\text{EBIT}) = [P(1 - S) - U - V]\Delta Q.$$

Our results are off by the change in fixed costs in inventory under absorption costing. Presumably, the firm would get back to equilibrium—sales equaling production—in a quarter or so.

Correspondingly, the change in total assets would involve all variable current asset components, because these change with unit volume. This change is

$$\Delta(\text{total assets}) = \left(\frac{PS + U + V}{t_c} + \frac{P}{t_a} + \frac{R}{t_r} + \frac{V}{t_i}\right)\Delta Q.$$

Thus, the new ROI, denoted by K_2, is

$$K_2 = \frac{(\text{Original EBIT}) + \Delta(\text{EBIT})}{(\text{Original total assets}) + \Delta(\text{Total assets})}$$

Figure 2-2 depicts the ROI-volume relationships for our HMD. The figure shows that ROI increases at a decreasing rate as a function of increases in volume (other things being equal).

Three additional points with respect to volume effects should be offered. First, note that "cash flow" for changes in volume for the period of the change is simply $\Delta(\text{EBIT}) - \Delta(\text{total assets})$, since no changes in fixed investment and depreciation are involved.

Throughout this book we will examine the impact of changes in costs, turnovers, and other factors in order to show how they affect cash flow in the period of the change. This change in cash flow is obviously important to the corporate treasury. In periods subsequent to the change, cash flow differs from that of the prior period by $\Delta(\text{EBIT})$. This is also important. For this purpose, we define *cash flow* as the change in profit minus the change in total investment, which is frequently negative, especially when managers seek higher volume through lower prices. This definition slightly misstates cash flow because part of the change in total investment consists of a change in the required cash balance – the amount that the operating unit needs to carry on its activities. Nevertheless, this cash balance ties up cash just as

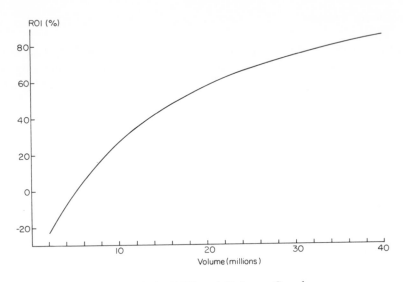

Figure 2-2. ROI and Volume Graph

receivables and inventory do, in the sense that the firm cannot use the cash for other investments. We therefore speak of a funds flow as essentially a flow of "free cash."

Because we will discuss the effects of changes in variables on "funds flow," we should be precise about the meaning. Essentially, we assume that the division turns over to the corporation the cash that it generates in excess of the balance it holds, if any. The effect on funds flow, then, is the difference between the amounts that the division could turn over under the original and the changed operating conditions, respectively. This effect is for the period of the change only. At equilibrium, with no growth, the division should generate cash equal to EBIT plus depreciation because asset requirements should not change. Actions or changes created from outside the division that change EBIT will change funds flow in later periods by the change in EBIT (holding depreciation constant). However, the period of the change shows a different effect—a one-shot increase or decrease in cash turned over to the corporation—and this effect is what we mean by "change in funds flow."

Subsequent chapters will treat changes in many variables, for some of which the "change in profit less change in investment" model wil. misstate funds flow. Appendix 2A covers these important exceptions. The change in "funds flow" predicted by a change in volume is then given by the following expression.

$$\Delta(\text{Funds}) = \left[P(1 - S) - U - V - \left(\frac{PS + U + V}{t_c} + \frac{P}{t_a} + \frac{R}{t_r} + \frac{V}{t_i} \right) \right] \Delta Q$$

In general, the selling price might be low enough that the first-period funds flow will be negative when volume increases, requiring that the firm put additional cash input into the division, plant, or product.

Second, note that there is an incremental ROI defined by $\Delta(\text{EBIT})/\Delta(\text{total assets})$, which also serves as the theoretical limit of ROI. Thus,

$$\text{Maximum ROI} = \frac{P(1 - S) - U - V}{\dfrac{PS + U + V}{t_c} + \dfrac{P}{t_a} + \dfrac{R}{t_r} + \dfrac{V}{t_i}}.$$

The maximum ROI for our HMD is 134.7 percent, which is also the incremental ROI per unit of volume at a constant $30.00 selling price. Third, note that figures 2-1 and 2-2 serve as combination breakeven charts and guides to ROI.

We can perform a similar analysis on price effects, as depicted in figure 2-3 (the figure assumes a volume of 15 million units). For price changes, denoted by ΔP,

$$\Delta(\text{EBIT}) = Q(1 - S)\Delta P,$$

$$\Delta(\text{Total assets}) = Q(S/t_c + 1/t_a)\Delta P,$$

$$\Delta(\text{Funds}) = Q(1 - S - S/t_c - 1/t_a)\Delta P.$$

Note that price increases are likely, but not guaranteed, to result in positive funds flows. The only current assets affected by price changes are cash (through increases in variable selling expenses, QPS) and receivables, whereas increases in volume affect all current assets. Later chapters show clearly and explicitly that seeking increased volume by reducing price can be a very risky strategy, and a very costly one for the corporate treasury. As a preview of pricing considerations, the reader can observe that a decrease in price without increases in volume has nasty effects on ROI, particularly at high levels of output (constant volume is assumed in figure 2-3). Thus, the price follower that must sometimes cut price just to maintain volume is at a distinct disadvantage.

As a final brief illustration, we might observe the effects on ROI of changes in accounts receivable turnover. For illustrative purposes we assume, unrealistically, that a change in the collection period affects only current assets, not volume, revenue, or EBIT. Typically, changes in turnovers are *results* of changes in credit checking or credit terms, which usu-

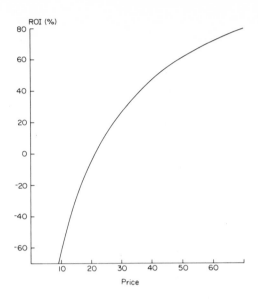

Figure 2-3. ROI and Price Graph

ally affect volume and, therefore, profit. (Chapters 4 and 5 deal extensively with tradeoffs involving credit terms, volume, prompt-payment discounts, and price.) The change in total assets for a change in accounts receivable turnover from t_{a1} to t_{a2} is given by

$$\Delta(\text{Total assets}) = \frac{-QP}{t_{a1}\,t_{a2}}\,\Delta t_a.$$

Therefore, the change in funds flow, in the current period, would be given by

$$\Delta(\text{Funds}) = \frac{QP}{t_{a1}t_{a2}}\,\Delta t_a.$$

The relationship between ROI and accounts receivable turnover is depicted in figure 2-4, which shows that when accounts receivable turnover is very low, small increases have significant impacts on ROI. Subsequent improvements in turnover have less-significant effects.

Table 2-2 summarizes the effects on EBIT and total assets of a change in any component. Inspection of this table is instructive and, given the particular set of circumstances faced by a particular firm, can be highly useful. However, such a set of change coefficients is per se quite sterile. Individual

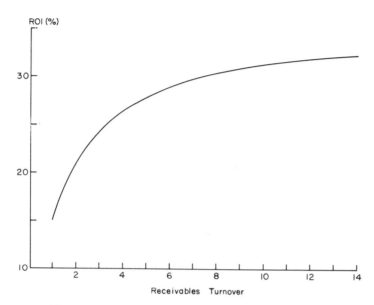

Figure 2-4. ROI and Receivables Turnover Graph

components of ROI rarely change independently; rather, changes in one component usually accompany changes in another. In fact, most actions taken by managers will affect more than one component, although not necessarily in the expected way. For example, tightening credit terms increases receivable turnover and probably reduces unit volume and bad debts (part of S). Subsequent chapters discuss such tradeoffs, which are extremely important in managing ROI.

One benefit of quantifying the relationships among various components of ROI is that it enables one to determine which variables are the critical ones—those that most significantly affect ROI. Managers can then concentrate on improving these variables—getting the most bang for the buck. The change coefficients are valuable for such analyses and also are helpful in developing policy statements. Further, they permit better evaluations of proposals than do existing methods. We consider these important matters throughout the rest of the book.

Viewpoint of the Analysis

It is always difficult to describe how to use analytical tools. Usually, the problem lies in trying to determine the reader's point of view in order to

Table 2-2
Change Relationships

EBIT Component: Price (P)	Δ Component: $\Delta P = P_2 - P_1$	Δ(EBIT): $Q(1-s)\Delta P$	Δ(Total Assets): $Q(S/t_c + 1/t_a)\Delta P$
Volume	$\Delta Q = Q_2 - Q_1$	$[P(1-s) - U - V]\Delta Q$	$\left(\dfrac{PS + U + V}{t_c} + \dfrac{P}{t_a} + \dfrac{R}{t_r} + \dfrac{V}{t_i}\right)\Delta Q$
Raw-materials cost (R)	$\Delta R = R_2 - R_1$	$-Q\Delta R$	$Q\left(\dfrac{1}{t_c} + \dfrac{1}{t_r} + \dfrac{1}{t_i}\right)\Delta R$
Other variable manufacturing cost (V')	$\Delta V' = V'_2 - V'_1$	$-Q\Delta V'$	$Q\left(\dfrac{1}{t_c} + \dfrac{1}{t_i}\right)\Delta V'$
Fixed manufacturing cost (F)	$\Delta F = F_2 - F_1$	$-\Delta F$	$(1/t_c + 1/t_i)\Delta F$
Variable unit selling expenses (U)	$RU = U_2 - U_1$	$-Q\Delta U$	$(Q/t_c)\Delta U$
Variable revenue selling expenses (S)	$\Delta S = S_2 - S_1$	$-QP\Delta S$	$(QP/t_c)\Delta S$
Fixed general and selling expenses (F')	$\Delta F' = F'_2$	$-\Delta F'$	$(1/t_c)\Delta F'$
Cash turnover (t_c)	$\Delta t_c = t_{c2} - t_{c1}$	0	$-\dfrac{(QPS + QU + QV + F + F')}{t_{c1}t_{c2}}\,\Delta t_c$
Accounts receivable turnover (t_a)	$\Delta t_a = t_{a2} - t_{a1}$	0	$-\dfrac{QP}{t_{a1}t_{a2}}\,\Delta t_a$
Raw-materials turnover (t)	$\Delta t_r = t_{r2} - t_{r1}$	0	$-\dfrac{Q}{t_{r2}t_{r2}}\,\Delta R$
Other-inventory turnover (t_i)	$\Delta t_i = t_{i2} - t_{i1}$	0	$-\dfrac{(QV + F + mdI)}{t_{i1}t_{i2}}\,\Delta t_i$

make the discussion and illustrations most immediately relevant. Although this chapter briefly explored changes in ROI, the rest of the book takes the point of view that the managers of the division or firm have selected a target rate of return and are trying to determine how to achieve it given the vast array of possible strategies and tactics. The managers might then analyze various components of ROI such as prices, volume, credit terms, commissions, inventory policy, and so forth, and make interdependent decisions to try to achieve the target ROI. This is not the only possible viewpoint: We could equally well look at things with a view to increasing ROI. However, we adopt the former view for ease of exposition and because it provides a satisfactory framework for analysis.

One value of the viewpoint we use is that it lends itself readily to sensitivity analysis. We will often work with changes, such as how much additional volume the firm must obtain to maintain ROI in the face of a cost increase. We would not expect managers to interpret our results literally; instead, they should look at such results as the permissible, or required, bounds within which to make decision. Obviously, if the division can increase ROI because it can increase its volume beyond the ROI-maintaining level, then it should do so.

Summary

This chapter showed how managers can combine basic CVP components and turnovers to produce a comprehensive model of ROI that is manageable and adaptable to a wide range of firms or divisions. Any approach requires certain simplifying assumptions; here, we have adopted those of CVP analysis, including the assumption that sales and production are equal. The model allows the manager to determine the likely effects on ROI of specific changes in critical variables.

Because the model uses only CVP data and turnovers, it requires no information not readily obtainable from the typical accounting system. The model allows the user to define and measure ROI in virtually any way, including or excluding current liabilities, stating plant at gross or net book value or using replacement cost or price-level-adjusted figures. The model leads to straightforward ways to determine the effects on profit, ROI, total assets, and funds flow of changes in any variable.

Appendix 2A
Product Costing:
Effects on Income
and Investment

The target-ROI model gives an income figure that is based on variable costing and on the costs of the current period. It ignores the cost of the beginning inventory, which creates a difference between actual and model results when manufacturing costs and other variables change. We view the income that the model gives as a better indicator than the income that actual historical costing gives because the model income does not include paper profits due to the beginning inventory being at lower cost than the ending inventory, or to production not equaling sales.

This appendix outlines the effects of product-costing methods on income and investment under several different circumstances of changing volume, costs, and inventory turnover. In some cases the effects are relatively small, and in others they are large. We will assume that use of the first-in-first-out (FIFO) method. The weighted-average method generally would give smaller differences in the results of the model compared with actual costing results than does FIFO.

Before we proceed, we should state that any planning model that does not consider the nuances of product-costing techniques will misstate results unless it specifically provides for inventories according to the method that the firm uses. Such provisions have two important disadvantages. First, they can become analytically intractable, requiring complex equations, and ad hoc values. Second, and more important, they obscure the underlying relationships because they give the critical results (income, investment, ROI, funds flow) *for the period of the change only.* Thus, the results give "paper profits" (or losses) such as FIFO typically generates. Another common example is when increasing production increases income even with sales held constant (by deferring fixed production costs in inventory). The question is really not whether our model, or any other, gives results the same as those that will show up in the financial statements, but whether it provides information that is useful in planning and decision making. We are careful about showing how the results of our model differ from actual results so that the reader can asses the magnitudes of the differences himself.

First, we can express inventories and production as follows, in units.

Beginning inventory $= Q_1/t_{i1}$

Ending inventory $= Q_2/t_{i2}$

Production $= Q_2 + Q_2/t_{i2} - Q_1/t_{i1}$

where Q_1 = the initial planned volume; Q_2 = the new planned volume; t_{i1} = the initial turnover of work in process and finished goods; and t_{i2} = the new turnover.

The following expressions summarize the differences between FIFO absorption costing and the model for the HMD outlined in table 2–1.

	Model	*FIFO*
Ending inventory	$\dfrac{Q_2V_2 + F_2 + mdI_2}{t_{i2}}$	$\left(\dfrac{Q_2V_2 + F_2 + mdI_2}{Q_2 + Q_2/t_{i2} - Q_1/t_{i1}}\right)\left(\dfrac{Q_2}{t_{i2}}\right)$
Cost of sales	$Q_2V_2 + F_2 + mdI_2$	$\dfrac{Q_1V_1 + F_1 + mdI_1}{t_{i1}} + V_2\left(Q_2 + \dfrac{Q_2}{t_{i2}} - \dfrac{Q_1}{t_{i1}}\right)$

$$+ F_2 + mdI_2 \; -\left(\frac{Q_2V_2 + F_2 + mdI_2}{Q_2 + Q_2/t_{i2} - Q_1/t_{i1}}\right)\left(\frac{Q_2}{t_{i2}}\right)$$

The magnitudes of the differences depend on the data, but with constant turnovers the effects are relatively small. The following schedule shows the differences for the HMD described in chapter 2, with a 100-percent increase in volume, from 10 to 20 million units.

	Model	*Actual*	
	Results	*Results*	*Differences*
EBIT	$228.00	$226.86	$1.14
Inventory	52.56	51.42	1.14

The differences are trivial. Changes in turnover and in inventoriable costs are more complicated. The model misstates both profit and ending inventory when inventory turnover changes, but not by the same amounts. When manufacturing costs change, it misstates profit but states inventory correctly. Accordingly, in order to determine the precise values, one must go through the calculations. Even so, unless the changes are quite large, the misstatements are not likely to be large. The following schedule shows the model results and actual results for the HMD with a change in turnover (t_i) from 5 to 4 and an increase in cash fixed manufacturing costs from $50 million to $60 million. This is an extreme case, with both changes working in the same direction and being fairly sizable. At higher volume, the differences would be less.

	Model *Results*	*Actual* *Results*	*Differences*
EBIT	$66.0	$70.7	$4.7
Inventory	43.2	42.3	0.9

Unlike the differences associated with a change in volume, these differences do not balance. The reason is that the model ignores the costs in the beginning inventory, calculating current-period income using current-period costs. In this respect, the model results for income are similar to the results that the last-in-first-out (LIFO) method would give. (They are not necessarily the same, however.)

It should be remembered that these differences apply to the period of a change, and begin to reverse in the next period. Afterwards, the equilibrium results from the model will equal the actual results. For many divisions and firms the period would be a quarter or perhaps even a month, rather than a year. This depends on how rapidly the manufacturer builds up or reduces inventory.

Changes in Manufacturing Costs

The following income statements show the differences between model results and actual results for the HMD at 10 million units, with variable production costs increasing to $11 per unit and fixed production costs requiring cash disbursements rising to $60 million.

	Model *Results*	*Actual* *Results*
Sales	$300.0	$300.0
Cost of sales ($QV + F + mdI$)	182.8	
(see later)		178.8
Gross margin	117.2	121.2
Selling and administrative expenses	61.2	61.2
Profit before taxes	$56.0	$ 60.0
Cost of sales calculation:		
Beginning inventory		$32.56
Production costs ($11 × 10 million + $60 + $12.8)		182.80

	Model Results	Actual Results
Available for sale		215.36
Ending inventory ($182.80/10 million × 2 million)		36.56
Cost of sales, actual FIFO		$178.80

The difference in incomes occurs because the model uses production costs for 10 million units, the quantity made and sold, as cost of sales. Income under the model does not benefit from the FIFO effect—the paper profits that actual historical costs give. Although the model results in this case are LIFO, because production equals sales, in other circumstances they would be a mixture of LIFO and replacement cost. This is an advantage because, as previously mentioned, FIFO (as well as weighted average) gives unduly optimistic (or pessimistic, if costs decline) results in the period of the change, obscuring the long-term effects on profits.

Funds Flow

This section explores some of the effects on first-period funds flow of the differences between model and actual results. In most cases, the Δ(EBIT) − Δ(total assets) does not give the actual flow. In general, the differences between the model results and actual results relate to the model's showing changes in fixed costs in inventory. These changes affect inventory and, therefore, the change in investment, but do not similarly affect the change in profit. First, if volume changes, and production changes along with it enough to maintain inventory turnover, then the difference between cash production costs and the quantity QV is simply unit variable cost times the difference between production and sales, in units. The model calculates inventory as:

$$\text{Inventory} = \frac{QV + F + mdI}{t_i}.$$

Therefore, the fixed costs in inventory under the model are constant as long as volume is the only changing variable. The differences between the model results for income and inventory and the actual results offset so that funds flow is correct. The change in inventory given by the model, with the concomitant change in production, is all variable costs. Cash payments for variable production costs are:

$$V(Q_2 + Q_2/t_i - Q_1/t_i),$$

or,

$$VQ_2 + V(Q_2/t_i - Q_1/t_i).$$

The first term is included in profit, and the second term is the increase in variable costs in inventory as given by the model. Thus, cash flows for production costs are captured by Δ(EBIT) $-$ Δ(total assets), when volume is the only changing variable.

However, when turnover changes, the model gives a change in fixed costs in inventory. This change does not affect funds flow, even though it shows up as a change in investment. Accordingly, to determine funds flow we must add the change given by the model to the quantity Δ(EBIT) $-$ Δ (total assets). The adjustment is simply

$$\frac{F + mdI}{t_{i1}} - \frac{F + mdI}{t_{i2}},$$

or

$$(F + mdI)\frac{t_{i2} - t_{i2}}{t_{i1}t_{i2}}.$$

Adding this difference to the change in profit minus the change in investment gives the correct funds flow. (If turnover decreases, then the value will be negative, reflecting a reduction that the model would show for fixed costs in inventories.)

Cost Changes

If fixed manufacturing costs requiring cash, F, change, then the model misstates cash flow by $\Delta F/t_i$ because the additional fixed costs do require cash, but an amount equal to $\Delta F/t_i$ will be inventoried *and* ΔF will be reflected in profit. If costs increase, then the cash outflow is overstated, and vice versa. If depreciation is allocated to plant changes, then the misstatement is $\Delta(mdI)(1 + 1/t_i)$ because the change in depreciation shows up as reduced profit, whereas the amount of the change inventoried shows up as an increase in investment. Neither affects cash.

Finally, if variable manufacturing costs, other than raw materials, change, then the model states inventory correctly but misstates income and funds flow by

$$\frac{-Q\,\Delta V}{t_i}\,.$$

Again, this effect occurs because the model ignores the beginning inventory.

3

Target-ROI Pricing

Pricing is exceedingly complex and is the subject of much sophisticated and exotic quantitative analysis. The methods developed in this chapter and the next rely only on the basic ROI model. We do not use demand curves, market-share models, or economic analyses. We do not claim to show how to *maximize* ROI or profit, or how to optimize some combination of objectives. Our principal objective is simple: to present an approach that managers can use to set and evaluate prices in reference to a target ROI.

Managers have known for many years that the pricing decision is iterative and subjective. More recently, many managers have begun to understand that ROI is an important consideration in pricing.[1] We take the view that pricing decisions cannot be separated from investment decisions, and we also acknowledge the subjective, iterative nature of the process. We do not consider the subjective analyses, important though they are, but concentrate on the investment decision. ROI is a fundamental criterion for evaluating the feasibility of a target price. Nevertheless, we know of only one approach to target ROI pricing: the General Motors (GM) model, first published in 1927. This model appears in appendix 3A.

The methods that follow, therefore, are primarily *target* pricing methods. They yield product prices that will achieve a given ROI objective provided that the estimates of other variables are accurate. From time to time we will discuss whether or not competitive and regulatory reality allow the firm to achieve the required volume at the target price; but these questions, although critical, are essentially outside the framework of our objectives.

Developing Target-ROI Pricing Methods

Once the managers of the firm or division have estimated the elements of profit and investment, as described in chapter 2 (except for price) and have selected a satisfactory target ROI, they can determine the target price. We could solve the basic equation from chapter 2 for price, but a simpler and quite satisfactory pricing model takes the form

Target price $= P =$ (Average cash manufacturing cost)$C + C_q$,

which simply states that the target-ROI price is the average out-of-pocket manufacturing cost for a given level of volume times a constant (C) plus a constant that varies with volume (C_q). Average cash manufacturing cost is given by

$$\text{Average cash manufacturing cost} = \frac{QV + F}{Q}.$$

The factors C and C_q may be algebraically threatening, but they are easy to understand and work with.

$$C = \frac{1 + K(1/t_c + 1/t_i)}{1 - S - K(S/t_c + 1/t_a)},$$

$$C_q = \frac{U(1 + K/t_c) + KR/t_r + [F' + dI + K(F'/t_c + mdI/t_i + I)]/Q}{1 - S - K(S/t_c + 1/t_a)}$$

The meaning of the denominator of both C and C_q is quite simple. It is the percentage of each dollar of revenue that is left over after covering variable revenue-based S, G, and A expenses and providing the target ROI on (1) the cash tied up by selling expenses and (2) receivables. This percentage of revenue is available to meet other expenses and to provide the target ROI on other investment. Notice that, in both C and C_q, this term is essentially multiplied by volume, Q (after some algebra in C_q). The term $1 - S - K(S/t_c + 1/t_a)$ is conveniently referred to as the *price-change coefficient* because one must consider it any time one is working with price or with a change in price.

The numerator of C simply states that price must cover total cash manufacturing costs ($QV + F$) and yield a return of K on cash and in-process and finished goods inventory generated by total cash manufacturing cost. Note, therefore, that C is independent of the level of volume.

The numerator of C_q requires recovery of unit selling and administrative expenses plus a return on cash tied up by these expenses. Further, a return on raw materials inventory must be earned. Finally, all fixed costs (exclusive of cash manufacturing costs) must be covered and a return of K generated on the cash tied up by fixed selling expenses (F'/t_c), depreciation in inventory (mdI/t_i), and plant and equipment (I). Because we want a unit price, we divide the last term by volume.

After calculating a target price using the equation, one is able to estimate all the components of profit and investment. The method lends itself well to iteration and tabulation over wide ranges of volume and yields a wealth of information for planning and analysis.

Target Pricing and Volume Analysis

In order to give a preliminary illustration of the target-ROI pricing method, we return to the hypothetical manufacturing division (HMD) from chapter 2. The division seeks a 40-percent ROI. Other pertinent information, except for product price, appears in table 2-1.

We begin by illustrating the calculation of a target price necessary to achieve this ROI for various volumes. This is given in table 3-1. As volume increases, average cash manufacturing cost decreases at a decreasing rate— falling rapidly at first, then much more slowly at greater levels of volume. (This is not a learning effect but simply the absorption of fixed manufacturing costs. A learning effect implies that variable manufacturing cost V also decreases with increasing volume.) Since C is a constant for all levels of assumed volume, this decreasing cost may be passed through, thus lowering the target price. Further, C_q also decreases with volume, with a similar impact on target price. The behavior of average cash manufacturing cost C, C_q, and target price appear in figure 3-1. Figure 3-2 gives price curves for three target ROIs.

The information in table 3-1 and figures 3-1 and 3-2 provides sound guidance for various strategic considerations. One obvious point is that maintaining or increasing ROI by reducing price to increase volume is much easier at low levels of volume than at high levels. By "easier," we mean that, as volume rises, the required percentage increase in volume is much higher for a given percentage decrease in price. The steepness of the curve at low volumes and its flatness at high volumes show this.

Table 3-1
Calculation of a 40-Percent Target-ROI Price

Volume (Millions)	Average Cash Manufacturing Cost (Dollars)	C	C_q (Dollars)	P (Dollars)
2	35.00	1.3914	60.38	109.08
4	22.50		31.45	62.76
6	18.33		21.81	47.32
8	16.25		16.99	39.60
10	15.00		14.10	34.97
12	14.17		12.17	31.88
14	13.57		10.79	29.67
16	13.13		9.76	28.02
18	12.78		8.95	26.73
20	12.50		8.31	25.70

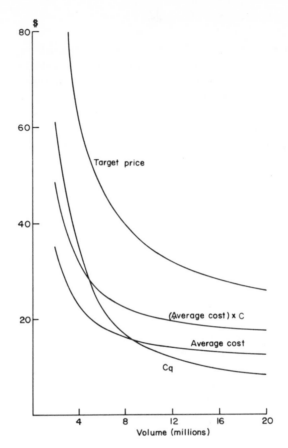

Figure 3-1. Target Price and Estimated Volume

Let us consider three situations. First, suppose that the product is a new, proprietary venture. If the HMD wanted to introduce the product slowly, at a high price, and then rapidly decrease the price in subsequent years to gain increased acceptance, it could examine the magnitude of price changes and volume requirements from table 3–1 or figure 3–1. Of course, in planning for years beyond the first, the managers would take inflation and other factors into account, perhaps by preparing price curves based on estimated costs and turnovers in future years.

Second, suppose that the product is new, but not proprietary. The division might want to gain as much of the new market as rapidly as possible to discourage competition. Once the product gains a high market share, there is not likely to be much opportunity to increase volume by lowering price,

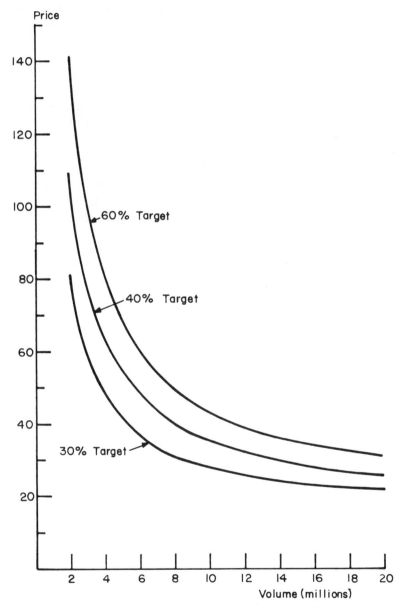

Figure 3-2. Price-Volume Relationships for Three Target ROIs

while still maintaining ROI. The flatness of the curve shows why. A manager already operating at high volume who tries to secure even higher vol-

ume by reducing prices must be *very* successful if he is not to suffer a decline in ROI.

Third, suppose that this product already competes with many others in the marketplace. Table 3-1 and figure 3-1 provide a framework for analyzing how much additional volume must accrue from a price reduction to gain market share. (The reverse is also possible. Increasing prices and reducing market share could well prove wise.) Such an analysis must be accomplished, of course, by an evaluation of potential reactions of competitors.

Graphs like figures 3-1 and 3-2 are valuable in analyzing alternatives because managers usually have some reasonable ideas of how price and volume are likely to be related even though they do not draw demand curves or formulate market-share models. Managers would generally work with fairly small parts of the curves, representing their relevant ranges. Within these ranges, they would probably be able to specify, quite accurately in many cases, what volume they could expect at a given price.

Basically, target pricing methods such as this provide a starting position for pricing decisions. Further "what if" analysis is clearly necessary and is even more beneficial when one compares the present approach with classical ROI methods. For managers studying price-volume relationships, the price graphs in figures 3-1 and 3-2 are valuable. (Any point on figure 3-2, whether or not it lies on a particular existing curve, represents a price-volume combination that will provide *some* ROI. The ROI could, of course, be very low or even negative. Managers who have some fairly strong convictions about price-volume relationships can look for combinations that would produce higher ROIs.)

The *model* underlying figures 3-1 and 3-2 is important and instructive. Suppose that a manager belives that he can increase volume by a specific amount if he reduces price. He wants to determine how much of a price reduction he can stand, meaning that he wants at least to maintain ROI. (Of course, the reverse is possible. He might want to increase price and accept a lower volume.) When the expected change in volume is $\Delta Q = Q_2 - Q_1$, the change in price required to maintain the target ROI is

$$\Delta P = -\frac{P_1(1 - S) - U - V - K[(P_1 S + U + V)/t_c + P_1/t_a + R/t_r + V/t_i]}{1 - S - K(S/t_c + 1/t_a)}$$

$$\left(\frac{\Delta Q}{Q_2}\right),$$

where ΔP is the required change, $P_2 - P_1$.

The denominator defining the required change in price, ΔP, is the *price-change coefficient,* which, of course, is the denominator of the price coefficients, C and C_q.

Similarly, the numerator is what we have already labeled the *volume-*

change coefficient, described in chapter 2. It will appear in any model relating a change in volume to any other component of the target ROI.

Suppose that the HMD, desiring a target ROI of 40 percent, wants to develop a simple application of the preceding formula. Its managers might start by assuming a given volume, say 16 million units, and work from that. Since the target price at 16 million units is $28.02, as given in table 3–1, the model could be stated as

$$\Delta P = -\$11.58(\Delta Q/Q_2),$$

and

$$P_2 = P_1 - \frac{\$11.58(Q_2 - 16)}{Q_2}.$$

This model provides a very simple target-ROI pricing equation that relates required price to a departure from the starting-point volume. Such an approach is most applicable and instructive once managers have determined the required price at a particular level of volume and want to experiment to see what changes in price would give the target ROI as they move volume away from the starting point. Developing a price based on an assumed level of volume is a commonplace practice (the GM model is one good example). Understanding the relationship between changes in the assumed volume and changes in the price is likely to prove very beneficial. (The GM model cannot provide this without major alterations, as appendix 3A shows). It is surely not uncommon for managers to decide that the required price at the first assumed level of volume is too high to permit achieving the volume. A trial-and-error search is much more efficient when the new required price is easily calculated at the new level of assumed volume, taking into immediate consideration the changes in investment that accompany changes in price and volume.

Table 3–2 outlines this relationship. Certainly, reductions in output as a result of weak demand rarely go hand in hand with price increases. Thus, we reiterate that these are target-ROI prices. If a drop in demand occurs with no change in price, the methods of chapter 2 show the effects on ROI.

Target Pricing, Volume, and Operating Results

Relating target-ROI pricing and volume analysis to expected operating results, for which *some* manager is invariably held accountable, is a necessary step in the overall pricing decision. Such items as total revenue, gross margin, net margin, total managed (current) assets, and ROI all vary with price decisions. Table 3–3 outlines income-statement results that should occur at various levels of volume.

Table 3–2
Price Changes Required by Changes in Assumed Volume (40-Percent Target ROI)

Q (Millions)	*ΔQ (Millions)*	*\$11.58ΔQ/Q (Dollars)*	P_2 *(Dollars)*
2	−14	−81.05	109.07
4	−12	−34.74	62.76
6	−10	−19.30	47.32
8	− 8	−11.58	39.60
10	− 6	− 6.95	34.97
12	− 4	− 3.86	31.88
14	− 2	− 1.65	29.67
16	0	0	28.02
18	2	1.29	26.78
20	4	2.32	25.70
22	6	3.16	24.86
24	8	3.86	24.16
26	10	4.45	23.57
28	12	4.96	23.06
30	14	5.40	22.62

Two observations can be made easily from an inspection of table 3–3. First, note that when target-ROI pricing is employed, changes in volume lead to nonlinear changes in price, but to simple linear changes in revenue and profit. Essentially, the change in total revenue, $\Delta(QP)$, when price also changes to maintain the target ROI, is given by

$$\Delta(QP) = \Delta(\text{Revenue}) = \text{Constant}\ \Delta Q,$$

$$\text{Constant} = \frac{U + V + K[V(1/t_c + 1/t_i) + U/t_c + R/t_r]}{1 - S - K(S/t_c + 1/t_a)}.$$

The constant is unit variable cost plus the required return on current assets that vary with these costs, divided by the price-change coefficient. This equation states that when output changes by ΔQ, revenue should change by ΔQ times a simple constant if price is changed to maintain the target ROI. This relationship can be derived easily from the original pricing equation. For our HMD we would have

$$\text{Constant} = \$16.44$$

Table 3-3
Cost-Volume-Profit Relationships with 40-Percent Target-ROI Price

Volume (Millions)	Price (Dollars)	Revenue (Millions)	Cost of Sales (Millions)	Gross Profit (Millions)	Percent- age Gross Margin	S,G,A (Millions)	EBIT (Millions)	Percent- age EBIT Margin
2	109.08	$218.15	$ 82.80	$135.35	0.620	$ 40.20	95.16	0.436
4	62.76	251.03	102.80	148.23	0.590	46.81	101.42	0.404
6	47.32	283.92	122.80	161.12	0.568	53.43	107.69	0.379
8	39.60	316.80	142.80	174.00	0.549	60.05	113.95	0.360
10	34.97	349.68	162.80	186.88	0.534	66.66	120.22	0.344
12	31.88	382.56	182.80	199.76	0.522	73.28	126.48	0.331
14	29.67	415.45	202.80	212.65	0.512	79.90	132.75	0.320
16	28.02	448.33	222.80	225.53	0.503	86.52	139.01	0.310
18	26.73	481.21	242.80	238.41	0.495	93.13	145.28	0.302
20	25.70	514.09	262.80	251.29	0.489	99.75	151.54	0.295
22	24.86	546.97	282.80	264.17	0.483	106.37	157.81	0.288
24	24.16	579.86	302.80	277.06	0.478	112.98	164.07	0.283
26	23.57	612.74	322.80	289.94	0.473	119.60	170.34	0.278
28	23.06	645.62	342.80	302.82	0.469	126.22	176.60	0.274
30	22.62	678.50	362.80	315.70	0.465	132.84	182.87	0.270

and

$$\Delta(\text{Revenue}) = \$16.44\Delta Q.$$

(ΔQ is stated in millions of units.) Thus, when it uses target-ROI pricing, each time the HMD increases volume by 1 million units, it should increase revenue by $16.44 million. Similarly, the change in earnings before interest and taxes, denoted by $\Delta(\text{EBIT})$, that occurs when volume changes by ΔQ is

$$\Delta(\text{EBIT}) = [\text{Constant}(1 - S) - U - V]\Delta Q.$$

This relationship should be fairly obvious, since any change in revenue equal to (constant) $\Delta(Q)$ will be reduced by all variable costs in determining EBIT. For the HMD,

$$\Delta(\text{EBIT}) = \$3.13\Delta Q.$$

(ΔQ is stated in millions of units.)

The second important observation in table 3-3 is the behavior of return on sales, labeled "Percentage EBIT Margin," in the last column. It can be seen that increases in volume yield decreases in the return on sales. An astonishing number of otherwise sophisticated managers persist in pricing based on return on sales even when their bonuses depend on ROI performance. Even the classical margin-times-turnover approach to ROI should inhibit that type of thinking. Yet it persists.

It is hard to quarrel with a manager who shows impressive results by pricing based on return on sales, target market share, or some other incomplete objective. Nevertheless, for all its faults, ROI is the principal criterion for evaluating divisional managers and corporate managers (indirectly through return on equity, earnings growth, dividend yield, and so forth); in competitive markets, the manager who concentrates on a partial measure of success is likely to be only partially successful.

The increases in total asset turnover that accrue from increases in volume appear in table 3-4. Here again, when target ROI pricing is employed, changes in total assets are a simple linear function of changes in output. This relationship is modeled by

Table 3-4
Balance-Sheet Relationships with 40-Percent Target-ROI Price
(units and dollars in millions)

Volume	Cash and Equivalents	Accounts Receivable	Raw-Materials Inventory	In-Process and Finished Inventory	Total Assets	Total Asset Turnover
2	$ 4.46	$ 54.54	$ 2.33	$16.56	$237.89	0.917
4	5.57	62.76	4.67	20.56	253.56	0.990
6	6.68	70.98	7.00	24.56	269.22	1.055
8	7.79	79.20	9.33	28.56	284.88	1.112
10	8.89	87.42	11.67	32.56	300.54	1.164
12	10.00	95.64	14.00	36.56	316.20	1.210
14	11.11	103.86	16.33	40.56	331.86	1.252
16	12.22	112.08	18.67	44.56	347.53	1.290
18	13.33	120.30	21.00	48.56	363.19	1.325
20	14.44	128.52	23.33	52.56	378.85	1.357
22	15.55	136.74	25.67	56.56	394.52	1.386
24	16.66	144.96	28.00	60.56·	410.18	1.414
26	17.77	153.18	30.33	64.56	425.84	1.439
28	18.88	161.41	32.67	68.56	441.52	1.462
30	19.98	169.63	35.00	72.56	457.17	1.484

$$\Delta(\text{Total assets}) = \left[\text{Constant }\left(\frac{S}{t_c} + \frac{1}{t_a}\right) + V\left(\frac{1}{t_c} + \frac{1}{t_i}\right) + \frac{U}{t_c} + \frac{R}{t_r}\right]\Delta Q,$$

where the constant is defined just as before. The interpretation is straightforward. Revenue increases by (constant) ΔQ, so that cash and receivables, which vary with revenue, change by $(\text{constant})(S/t_c + 1/t_a)\,\Delta Q$. Further, other elements of current assets that vary with volume change by $V(1/t_c + 1/t_i)\,\Delta Q$ for variable manufacturing cost tied up in cash and in finished and in-process inventories; by $(U/t_c)\,\Delta Q$ for cash holdings related to variable selling expenses; and by $(R/t_r)\,\Delta Q$ for changes in raw materials and purchased components. For the HMD,

$$\Delta(\text{Total assets}) = \$7.83\Delta Q.$$

The effect on funds flow for changes in volume, given target-ROI pricing, is therefore a direct result since no change in depreciation is involved. Thus, we determine funds flow (or cash flow) exactly as in chapter 2:

$$\Delta(\text{Funds}) = \Delta(\text{EBIT}) - \Delta(\text{Total assets}).$$

For this case,

$$\Delta(\text{Funds}) = \left[\text{Constant }\left(1 - S - \frac{S}{t_c} - \frac{1}{t_a}\right) - V\left(1 + \frac{1}{t_c} + \frac{1}{t_i}\right)\right.$$
$$\left. - U\left(1 + \frac{1}{t_c}\right) - \frac{R}{t_r}\right]\Delta Q,$$

where the constant maintains the same definition. For our division,

$$\Delta(\text{Funds}) = -\$4.70\Delta Q.$$

Thus, increases in volume predict negative flows of funds during the first period, a result that the attentive reader would expect. In chapter 2 we saw that increases in volume with price constant could lead to negative funds flows. Here, price falls because we are using a target ROI, so that the effect on funds flow in the first period should be even worse. Obviously, a drop in price that does not lead to the required increase in volume produces even worse results, with high funds requirements and lower profit and ROI.

Table 3–4 also gives information about asset requirements. Each additional 2 million units yields a negative funds flow of $9.40 million, from the foregoing relationship. Certainly, there may be spontaneous sources of funds, such as trade payables and accruals that would cushion the shortfall. (This is true if the firm's target ROI is based on total assets, with no provision for current liabilities. If managers do gain the benefit of current liabilities in the investment base and incorporate that into the turnovers, then the increases in current assets are stated net of increases in current liabilities and the negative funds flow is stated net of short-term financing. In that case, the negative flow is net, and the firm must finance all of it externally.) Accordingly, this result dictates that, "If it's volume you want, see your banker."

Of course, to the extent that price increases can be achieved with reductions in volume, significant increases in cash flow can be attained while still maintaining the target ROI. A manufacturing division in the "harvest stage" is an obvious candidate for such a strategy.

Because divisions compete for corporate resources, one problem that corporate management continually faces is whether to treat a particular division as a "cash cow," a star performer, or something in between. The answer requires a long-range approach, and our single-period model is of limited benefit. However, the model does show that increasing volume for any division, while pricing to maintain a target ROI, is costly to the corporate treasury (as long as the target ROI is less than 100 percent, as we will see in chapter 5).

Figure 3–3 graphically illustrates the behavior of return on sales and total-asset turnover as a function of sales volume given target-ROI prices. Total-asset turnover, denoted t_{TA}, may be further decomposed into fixed-asset turnover, defined as sales divided by fixed assets and denoted t_{FA}, and current-asset turnover, defined as sales divided by total current assets and denoted t_{CA}. Then,

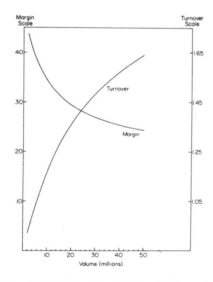

Figure 3–3. Margin and Turnover and Volume Changes with Target Pricing

$$t_{TA} = \frac{t_{CA} t_{FA}}{t_{CA} + t_{FA}}.$$

This relationship is outlined in figure 3–4.

Figure 3–4 highlights an interesting problem created by performance-evaluation methods the authors have encountered in some divisionalized firms. Some division managers are held accountable for return on "managed" assets, which typically do not include property, plant, and equipment. It is evident that the firm is maintaining a 40-percent return on total

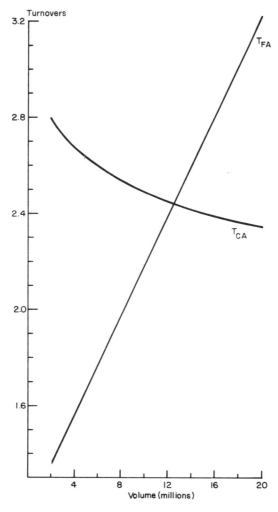

Figure 3–4. Turnovers and Volume with Target-ROI Pricing

assets with increases in volume, even though return on sales and turnover of managed (that is, current) assets are both declining. Defining return on managed assets as (EBIT margin) $\times t_{CA}$, we see that this return is 122 percent at a volume of 2 million units and drops to 69 percent at 20 million units.

Managers held responsible only for returns on current assets might make decisions that would increase their own ROIs while lowering the firm's overall ROI. They could be tempted to "skim the market," pricing high and accepting low volume to keep return on current assets high. Thus, ROI for divisional performance evaluation should be based on total divisional investment, unless measures are available to prevent the actions just described.

Target-ROI Pricing on the Learning Curve

Earlier in this chapter, in the discussion of average cash manufacturing cost data in table 3–1, we noted that the reduction in average manufacturing cost as volume increased was not a learning effect but simply the absorption of fixed costs of production. Yet one of the most powerful analytical tools in some industries is the learning curve, and the concept of *pricing on the learning curve* is currently popular. A learning effect implies that the unit variable cost of production V decreases with increasing volume. Our HMD has variable manufacturing costs of \$10 per unit, which we held constant at all levels of volume.

Incorporating learning effects into target-ROI pricing can be very complex. Two questions must be addressed before we go further. First, what components of variable manufacturing cost are candidates for learning effects? Are total variable costs affected, or only some component of total variable cost such as direct labor? Second, how are these learning effects to be measured and represented algebraically? For our first illustration, we assume that the per-unit cost of raw materials and purchased components is unaffected by increasing volume. Thus, we first treat the representation of total variable cost as $V = V' + R$, where V' is the nonmaterial component and is subject to learning effects.

As for algebraic representation, the classical learning curve is usually modeled as follows:

$$V' = B_0 Q^{B_1}$$

where Q is cumulative production (for our purposes, in millions of units); B_0 is the unit cost of the first unit (\$3.00 in our case); and B_1, a negative number, is the exponent, which is typically stated as

$$B_1 = \frac{\log \text{(Learning rate)}}{\log 2}.$$

The *learning rate* represents the amount of the reduction in average variable cost per unit as cumulative volume doubles. For instance, if the learning rate is 80 percent, then we say that average variable manufacturing cost drops 20 percent each time output doubles. Some representative values of B_1 would be:

Learning Rate	B_1
95%	-0.074
90	-0.152
85	-0.234
80	-0.322
75	-0.415
70	-0.515

Let us illustrate the target-ROI pricing model by using a 90-percent learning rate for our HMD and assuming that the $3.00 variable cost applies to the first 1 million units. Then the model would be:

$$P = \left(\frac{QV + F}{Q}\right)C + C_q,$$

$$P = \left[\frac{Q(V' + R) + F}{Q}\right]C + C_q,$$

$$V' = 3Q^{-0.152};$$

and C and C_q will be exactly the same as in table 3-1.

Our HMD, whose other variable manufacturing costs are subject to the learning curve outlined here, would now show 40-percent target-ROI prices, as outlined in table 3-5. Obviously, a firm with a greater proportion of costs subject to the learning effect would show much more dramatic results. Nevertheless, even though only 30 percent of the original variable manufacturing costs are subject to learning effects, the impact on unit costs and target prices with increasing volume is significant. Nonmaterial variable manufacturing costs have fallen from $3.00 to an average, over 20 million units, of $1.90. Average cash manufacturing cost has fallen by $1.10 and the target price by $1.50.

Additionally, we should point out that the learning effect has further

Table 3-5
Target-ROI Pricing: 90-Percent Learning Curve on Other Variable Manufacturing Costs

Volume (Millions)	Average Other Variable Cost	Average Variable Cost	Average Cash Manufacturing Cost	P
2	$2.70	$9.70	$34.70	$108.66
4	2.43	9.43	21.93	61.96
6	2.28	9.28	17.61	46.31
8	2.19	9.19	15.44	38.47
10	2.11	9.11	14.11	33.73
12	2.06	9.06	13.23	30.58
14	2.01	9.01	12.58	28.29
16	1.97	8.97	12.10	26.60
18	1.93	8.93	11.71	25.24
20	1.90	8.90	11.40	24.17

benefits in subsequent periods. Whereas the *average* variable manufacturing cost (excluding materials) for 20 million units in the current period is $1.90, the variable cost of the last unit produced is $1.61, and this cost carries through to the following planning period. In the next operating period, if another 20 million units are produced, the average variable manufacturing cost drops to $1.52 per unit ($8.52 including raw materials), and the 40-percent target-ROI price becomes $23.64, exclusive of inflation.

To the extent that learning also affects the per-unit cost of raw materials and purchased components, as it is reported to do in the semiconductor industry, application of the learning curve requires more computation. This is because, for a given volume, the value of raw materials inventory will decline with learning effects. Assuming a 90-percent learning rate applicable to all variable manufacturing costs (meaning, for the HMD, $V = 10Q^{-0.152}$), we get the target pricing results in table 3-6.

Contemporary corporate pricing strategy seems to have high regard for learning curves, especially in the electronics industries. We tend to believe that some proponents of this concept have oversold it in claiming that it applies to virtually all industries. It is clearly a significant factor in some industries, such as shipbuilding, aircraft manufacturing, and electronics. New-product pricing strategies are the most fruitful category for learning curves, but we tend to think that the planning horizon for such models is very short. The real benefits of volume are still the absorption of fixed costs and fixed investment.

Table 3-6
Target-ROI Pricing: 90-Percent Learning Curve on Total Variable
Manufacturing Cost

Volume (Q) (Millions)	R	V	$\dfrac{(QV + F}{Q}$	C	C_q	P
2	$6.30	$9.00	$34.00	1.3914	$60.32	$107.63
4	5.67	8.10	20.60		31.34	60.00
6	5.33	7.62	15.95		21.67	43.86
8	5.10	7.29	13.54		16.83	35.67
10	4.93	7.05	12.05		13.92	30.69
12	4.80	6.85	11.02		11.98	27.31
14	4.69	6.70	10.27		10.60	24.89
16	4.59	6.56	9.69		9.55	23.03
18	4.51	6.44	9.22		8.74	21.57
20	4.44	6.34	8.84	↓	8.10	20.40

Pro Forma Results and Sensitivity Analysis

An important byproduct of the target-ROI methods presented in this chapter is the construction of pro forma financial statements. Table 3-7 presents budgeted income-statement and balance-sheet figures for the HMD assuming target-ROI pricing at 10 million and 18 million units (no learning effects). The line items outlined in the table could then be employed, together with the methods given in table 2-2, for the analysis of operating variances. (Again, if current liabilities are incorporated into turnovers, then the figures shown for current assets are net of related liabilities. Appendix 3B shows the calculations of gross asset and liability amounts.)

Figure 3-5 highlights a particularly interesting type of sensitivity analysis. Actual ROI is plotted against actual volume expressed as a function of 40-percent target-ROI prices for various estimated volumes. Each curve in the figure represents actual ROI for each volume if the division priced to achieve a 40-percent ROI at the assumed level of volume. The calculations assume that the division adjusts inventories to meet the different volumes—that is, it maintains its turnovers. In practice, we might expect lower volume to be accompanied by lower turnover and higher-than-expected inventories, with correspondingly lower ROIs. Figure 3-5 then presents best-case results when actual volume is less than that used to set the price. Notice that for each price curve, if actual volume equals standard (assumed) volume, then the actual ROI is, of course, 40 percent. In our opinion, this type of figure offers a much more effective representation of price-volume results than

Table 3-7
Pro Forma Target-ROI Operating Results
(Millions)

	10 Million Units	18 Million Units
Income Statement		
Sales (*QP*)	$349.68	$481.21
Cost of sales		
Variable (*QV*)	100.00	180.00
Fixed (*F*)	50.00	50.00
Depreciation (*mdI*)	12.80	12.80
Gross profit	$186.88	$238.41
Selling, general, and administrative		
Unit variable (*QU*)	15.00	27.00
Revenue variable (*QPS*)	38.46	52.93
Fixed (*F*)	10.00	10.00
Depreciation [(1 − *m*)*dI*]	3.20	3.20
Earnings before interest and taxes	$120.22	$145.28
Balance Sheet		
Current assets		
Cash [(*QPS* + *QU* + *QV* + *F* + *F′*)/*t_c*]	$ 8.89	$ 13.33
Accounts receivable (*QP*/*t_a*)	87.42	120.30
Raw materials (*QR*/*t_r*)	11.67	21.00
Other inventory [(*QV* + *F* + *mdI*)/*t_i*]	32.56	48.56
Total current assets	$140.54	$203.19
Property, plant, and equipment	160.00	160.00
Total assets	$300.54	$363.19

classical breakeven graphs (breakeven levels, in terms of the target ROI, for each price curve are obvious in figure 3-5). Notice, also, that the algebraic representation for each curve in the figure can be found in the second row in table 2-2.

$$K_2 = \frac{\text{(Original EBIT)} + \Delta\text{(EBIT)}}{\text{(Original total assets)} + \Delta\text{(Total assets)}}.$$

It should be obvious that no division is likely to be able, say, to charge a price that would give a 40-percent ROI at an estimated volume of 2 million units and then to operate at, say, 14 million units. Many of the points on the curves are simply outside any reasonable range. Nevertheless, the results are instructive.

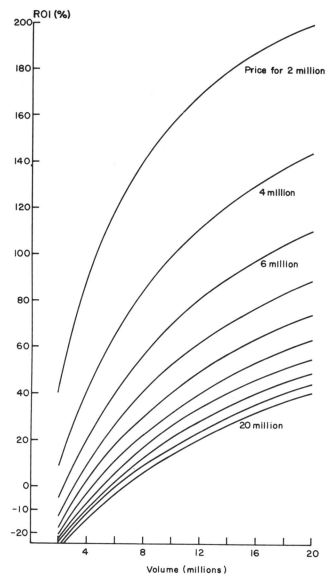

Figure 3–5. Actual ROIs for 40-Percent Target Prices at Assumed Volume

Summary

Utilizing the representation of return on investment developed in chapter 2, this chapter introduced the concept of target-ROI pricing. The basic method presented, that is,

$$P = (\text{Average cash manufacturing cost})\,C + C_q,$$

is very easy to work with and encompasses a wide range of applications such as price-volume analysis, funds-flow considerations, learning curves, pro forma computations, and sensitivity analysis.

Note

1. See, for example, Gilbert Burck, "Myths and Realities of Corporate Pricing," *Fortune,* April 1972, pp. 84–89.

Appendix 3A
The General Motors
Pricing Model

The General Motors (GM) model was published in the *NACA Bulletin* of 1 January 1927 by Albert Bradley, then general assistant treasurer and later chairman of the board. A more accessible source is the 4th edition of *Management Control Systems,* by Robert N. Anthony and John Dearden.[1]

The GM model is remarkable for its sophistication, its age notwithstanding. We can express it in our notation as follows.

$$K = \frac{QP(1 - S) - M}{\dfrac{M}{t_r} + \dfrac{M}{t_i} + \dfrac{M}{t_p} + \dfrac{QP}{t_a}},$$

where M = total manufacturing cost at the standard volume (Q); t_r = turnover of raw materials and work-in-process inventories (combined and based on total manufacturing cost); t_i = turnover of finished goods inventory; and t_p = turnover of plant and equipment (again based on total manufacturing cost). Cash and receivables are combined in t_a in the GM model.

Price is expressed as a multiple of average manufacturing cost,

$$P = \frac{M}{Q}\left[\frac{K/t_r + K/t_i + K/t_p}{1 - S - K/t_a}\right].$$

This formulation is easily derived from the schedule in Anthony and Dearden, *Management Control Systems.*[2] The model states a policy in the sense of a long-term target price; in some years the actual price could be higher, in some years lower. The model was applied to different products by allocating investment and costs to the individual products. The model was also meant to be used with a standard volume figure, so that, for example, it is possible to state plant and equipment using a turnover figure because the term M/t_p is constant as long as volume is constant.

The model has the following deficiencies:

1. It uses a single standard volume. If a manager wishes to change the standard volume, he must:
    a. recompute the turnover of fixed assets because they will not change in total if volume, and therefore total manufacturing cost, changes.
    b. recompute the turnover of raw materials unless they actually do turn over with total manufacturing costs, which seems unlikely.

2. The same problems arise if factory costs, either fixed or variable, change. Turnovers must then be recalculated.

3. The assumption that S,G,&A expenses can be expressed as a percentage of total revenue is very weak, essentially assuming that all S,G,&A expenses are variable. First, a good proportion of these expenses will be fixed, not variable at all. Second, the model solves for price at a given level of volume. Therefore, total revenue depends on the price for which one solves, which means that the assumption of a known percentage is a case of circular reasoning. (Even if one knows total S,G,&A expenses, one cannot determine their percentage relationship to sales unless one also knows the price per unit and the total volume. But one is solving the model for price using the percentage.)

Having said this, we still believe that the GM model is an extremely well-conceived one, given that it was meant to be used in conjunction with a standard volume figure.

Notes

1. Robert N. Anthony and John Dearden, *Management Control Systems,* 4th ed. (Homewood, Ill.: Richard D. Irwin, 1980).

2. Ibid., p. 97.

Appendix 3B
Pro Forma Results:
Gross Current Assets
and Liabilities

The turnovers for our HMD could have been either gross or net of related liabilities. The choice depends on whether or not the firm includes current liabilities in the investment base for which it holds operating managers responsible. Suppose that the firm does include current liabilities of two types: accruals and trade payables. Accruals are related to total cash disbursements, and trade payables are related to purchases of raw materials and components. The turnovers used in the illustration reflect these related liabilities, so that "cash" is really "cash less accruals" and "materials inventory" is really "materials inventory less trade payables."

This does no harm in determining the target price, but some managers would prefer to see the pro forma balance-sheet results stated gross, not net. This simply necessitates separating the assets from the related liabilities. In our example, the net turnover of cash less accruals was twenty-four times, and of materials less payables was six times. Innumerable combinations of turnovers of the assets and related liabilities would yield these net turnovers. We shall assume the following values.

Asset or Liability	Turnover
Cash	16
Accruals	48
Materials inventory	3
Trade payables	6

Using the formula given in the text, the net turnover of an asset and related liability is:

$$t_n = \frac{t_A t_L}{t_L - t_A}.$$

Using the gross turnovers would give the pro forma balance-sheet results shown in table 3B-1. The total investment figures are the same as those in table 3-7; only the makeups are different. For determining the target price, there is no reason not to combine assets and liabilities that turn over with the same measure of activity.

Table 3B–1
Gross Pro Forma Balance Sheets
(millions)

	10 Million Units	18 Million Units
Current assets		
Cash	$ 13.34	$ 20.00
Accounts receivable	87.42	120.30
Raw materials	23.33	42.00
In-process and finished goods	32.56	48.56
	$156.65	$230.86
Total current assets		
Current liabilities		
Accruals	$ 4.45	$ 6.67
Trade payables	11.67	21.00
Total current liabilities	$ 16.12	$ 27.67
Working capital	$140.53	$203.19
Property, plant, and equipment	160.00	160.00
Total investment	$300.53	$363.19

Some readers might wish to fine tune the basic model, incorporating, for example, a current liability that does not turn over the same measure of volume as does a current asset. For instance, a firm or division might have accruals related to manufacturing costs requiring cash, with all S,G,&A expenses paid as incurred. The liability could be expressed as:

$$\text{Accruals} = (QV + F)/t_\ell$$

where t_ℓ = the turnover of the accruals. The term would then be subtracted from the denominator of the basic ROI equation from chapter 2. The coefficient C would change to the following.

$$C = \frac{1 + K(1/t_c + 1/t_i - 1/t_\ell)}{1 - S - K(S/t_c + 1/t_a)},$$

and C_q would remain the same.

Remember that we have been working with turnovers that we believe are reasonable in the sense that the measure of activity is the most likely. If one's operations have assets or liabilities that turn over with different measures of activity, one need only modify the term describing the asset or liability, restate the basic equation, and re-solve for any analysis that is desired. In general, the form of the target-pricing equation will remain the same.

$$P = (\text{Average cash manufacturing cost})C + C_q.$$

4

Target-ROI Pricing Tactics

The material presented in chapters 1 through 3 outlined how managers can establish return-on-investment targets, how they can quantify the components of ROI operationally, and how they can use an operational definition to develop target-ROI pricing strategies. This chapter expands the previous material by outlining how managers can use these methods to change prices as environmental conditions or corporate policies change. In other words, this chapter concentrates on methods that managers can use to determine how much, or how little, they must change prices to maintain ROI in the face of changes in costs and turnovers. The set of relationships allows managers to determine their key factors—the ones that they must monitor closely.

At the outset, we reinforce two points that continue to guide our presentation. First, we are assuming that the firm is attempting to achieve a previously established target return on investment. It is not seeking to *maximize* profits, revenue, ROI, or the present value of stockholder wealth. Economically sound as some of these objectives might be, they require information that is simply not generally available. Our approach provides a set of ways of analyzing and planning using a target ROI and understanding the effects of decisions on ROI, revenue, profit, and cash flow. This approach is quite useful given that human endeavors rarely have a single objective.

Second, as observed in chapter 3, pricing tactics cannot really be separated from investment decisions and analyses of volume-price relationships. However, for the sake of parsimony of presentation, we have made such a separation. An all-at-once approach would not allow us to show how managers can respond to individual components. For example, if the firm changes its credit terms, it must expect the change to affect price or volume, or both. However, this chapter deals only with price effects, whereas chapter 5 deals with volume effects.

This chapter has three principal objectives: (1) to present methods for suggesting how a firm must change its target-ROI price in the face of changing operating costs; (2) to show how elements of policy (represented by changes in turnovers) affect the target ROI price and how these may interact with some cost components; and (3) to illustrate the concept of incremental pricing to achieve a target return on investment.

This chapter and those that follow use a good many algebraic expressions that relate a change in some variable (cost, turnover, plant assets) to a change in price or volume required to maintain the target ROI. It is always possible to determine the new required price by re-solving the basic equation from chapter 3 with the new value for the changed variable. However, the "change relationships" are valuable, for several reasons.

First, some useful policy statements flow from expressions of relationships of changes. One example given in this chapter shows that, for our HMD, an increase in certain manufacturing costs requires an increase in price of 139 percent of the cost increase to maintain ROI, when volume is held constant.

The second reason, related to the first, is that one continual job of managers is evaluating proposals of their peers and subordinates. Such proposals might involve cost increases, changes in credit policy that would change receivable turnover, and so on. The change relationships, even in very simple form, provide tools for spotting poorly conceived proposals very quickly. The example just given is again relevant. The HMD would not benefit by increasing price by $1.25 if it had to increase direct labor cost by $1.00 per unit (say, to increase quality) if volume remained constant. Hard analyses often reveal that some proposed strategies have little chance of success and should not be attempted. This point relates to one made earlier: Managers sometimes make proposals that are based on partial measures of success (return on sales, market share, and so forth). Those evaluating the proposals must look beyond the probable effects on the partial measure. Obviously, they must look beyond the effect on ROI in the short run; nevertheless, ROI is a crucial criterion. An action designed, say, to increase market share might be desirable in the long run; but the manager who decides whether or not to take the action must still be concerned with the short-run effects on profit, investment, ROI, and funds flow.

Third, the change relationships typically include several variables, reflecting the ripple effects of changes and interactions among different variables. For example, the increase in price required to maintain ROI in the face of a drop in raw materials turnover requires consideration not only of the additional inventory, but also of the additional cash and receivables that a higher selling price would cause. Looking at the change relationships helps managers to bear in mind those important interactions.

Finally, change relationships essentially deal with sensitivities. They show how sensitive a target price is to changes in other variables. Managers who have determined the relationships can then concentrate on the most crucial ones, for example, by requiring more frequent monitoring. This gets into the control function, which has not been discussed because the implications of the model for control are beyond the basic scope of the book.

Again, we stress that we are considering changes, and responses to them, in isolation. We acknowledge that managers faced with, say, increases in labor cost would search for several ways to mitigate the effects. They would look for combinations of price, volume, and other factors that would work. Moreover, changes do not occur one at a time either. However, for illustrative purposes there is no other reasonable way to proceed.

Changes in the Target-ROI Price and Changes in Costs

Organizations must continually monitor cost changes in order to adjust prices (if they can) to achieve a target ROI. Conceptually, whether the cost change is an increase or a decrease is of no significance. Practically, however, there is an enormous difference between a cost increase and a cost decrease. A firm would, or should, attempt to pass through a cost increase to maintain ROI; this is not necessarily true of a cost decrease. The comparison is further complicated by questions of volume changes, competitors' reactions, and possible regulatory constraints. Thus, we will first concentrate on cost increases and then turn to the question of cost decreases. If the firm is unable to pass through cost increases, its ROI will change in accordance with the coefficients given in table 2-2.

Passing Through Increases in Manufacturing Costs

Let us introduce the problem with the most basic of questions. Suppose that the firm experiences an increase in fixed manufacturing costs requiring cash, denoted $\Delta F = F_2 - F_1$. (We examine depreciation in chapter 6.) If the firm cannot increase its volume, then how much must it increase the target price to maintain ROI? Further, if the full price increase is achievable, what would be the impact on revenue, earnings before interest and taxes (EBIT), total assets, and funds flow?

One needs only to review the basic target-price relationship,

$$P = \left(\frac{QV + F}{Q}\right)C + C_q.$$

We can easily specify the required increase in the target price, denoted ΔP, when fixed manufacturing costs increase by ΔF. That is,

$$\Delta P = \frac{C\Delta F}{Q}.$$

The expression states that the required increase in the target-ROI price is equal to the change in fixed manufacturing costs spread over the given production volume and multiplied by the constant pricing coefficient, C. The reader will recall that

$$C = \frac{1 + K(1/t_c + 1/t_i)}{1 - S - K(S/t_c + 1/t_a)}.$$

The interpretation of C appeared in chapter 3, but it may be instructive to review these models by utilizing the following relationship.

$$Q[1 - S - K(S/t_c + 1/t_a)]\Delta P = [1 + K(1/t_c + 1/t_i)]\Delta F,$$

or

$$Q\Delta P(1 - S) - \Delta F = K[Q\Delta P(S/t_c + 1/t_a) + \Delta F(1/t_c + 1/t_i)],$$

$$\Delta(EBIT) = K\Delta(Total\ assets).$$

Note that the left-hand side of this equation is simply the change in EBIT. This change should be equal to the required return on those elements of current assets that vary with either the change in price or the change in fixed manufacturing costs. As price increases by ΔP, required cash balances increase by $(Q\Delta PS/t_c)$ and accounts receivable increase by $(Q\Delta P/t_a)$. As fixed manufacturing costs increase by ΔF, required cash balances increase by $(\Delta F/t_c)$ and in-process and finished goods inventory increases by $(\Delta F/t_i)$.

This understanding is important, but the principal point of this presentation is that a required change in target price is simply stated as

$$\Delta P = C(\Delta F/Q).$$

Of course, when volume is low, actually achieving the required price increase is quite another matter.

In order to illustrate the use of the relationship outlined here, let us return to the HMD introduced in chapter 2. There, C was equal to 1.3914, as first presented in table 3-1. Thus, if fixed manufacturing costs increased by 10 percent, from $50 million to $55 million, then the only remaining question is the assumed standard volume. The price increases for 10 million units and 18 million units are as follows.

	10 million units	18 million units
Original price	$34.97	$26.73
Increase in fixed costs	$5 million	$5 million
C	1.3914	1.3914
Increase in price	$ 0.69	$ 0.39
New price	$35.66	$27.12

These price increases, small though they are because of the illustrated volumes, do point out a major difference between classical profit-maximizing theories of the firm and a target-ROI approach. Under classical profit-maximizing theories, fixed costs are irrelevant in price determination. Few practicing managers would appreciate or agree with such a prescription. Under the target-ROI approach, however, price increases yield revenue increases greater than the increases in fixed costs because of the accompanying increases in current assets. This point will be greatly reinforced when we discuss variable cost increases.

The impact of an increase in fixed manufacturing costs and associated increase in price relative to revenue, EBIT, total assets, and funds flow becomes a simple matter once the required increase in the target price is understood. The relationships are:

$$\Delta(\text{Revenue}) = C\Delta F.$$

$$\Delta(\text{EBIT}) = [C(1 - S) - 1]\Delta F,$$

$$\Delta(\text{Total assets}) = [C(S/t_c + 1/t_a) + 1/t_c + 1/t_i]\Delta F,$$

$$\Delta(\text{Funds}) = \Delta(\text{EBIT}) - \Delta(\text{Total assets}).$$

Given previous discussions, it should come as no surprise that although the required target-price increase depends on volume, changes in revenue, EBIT, and total assets are strictly linear functions of the change in costs; they are not modified by volume. (Note that historical-cost-based product costing would give different results, by $\Delta F/t_i$, in the first operating period. In dealing with two points of equilibrium, it is preferable, for planning purposes, to leave the equations as they are. See appendix 2B for more on the general problem.)

Table 4–1 summarizes the effects on the components of ROI for our HMD given a $5-million increase in fixed manufacturing costs. Note that Δ (EBIT) divided by Δ(total assets) is still 40 percent, the firm's target ROI. Also, it is important to note that although the target ROI is main-

Table 4–1
Price Effects for an Increase in Fixed Manufacturing Costs

Initial Volume (Millions)	ΔP	P_2	Δ (Revenue) (Millions)	Δ (EBIT) (Millions)	Δ (Total Assets) (Millions)
2	$3.47	$112.55	$6.96	$1.19	$2.98
4	1.74	64.50			
6	1.16	48.48			
8	0.87	40.47			
10	0.69	35.66			
12	0.58	32.46			
14	0.50	30.17			
16	0.44	28.46			
18	0.39	27.12			
20	0.35	26.05	↓	↓	↓

Note: $\Delta F = \$5$ million.

tained, the cost increase, *even with the required price increase,* still yields a negative funds flow of $1.79 million. The ease with which one can use the target-ROI approach in predicting this need for funds is an important benefit. Also note that if ΔF represented a cost decrease, then a full pass-through of this decrease using target-ROI pricing would lower revenue, EBIT, and total assets while yielding a positive funds flow. This result is the reason that we are deferring cost reductions to a later section.

We must approach the required increase in the target-ROI price for increases in variable manufacturing cost by separating variable manufacturing cost (V) into raw materials and purchased components (R) and other variable manufacturing costs (V') such as direct labor. (Recall that $V = V' + R$.) Let us first look at an increase in other variable manufacturing cost, denoted $\Delta V'$, and the required increase in target price, ΔP. The relationship is

$$\Delta P = C\Delta V',$$

where C maintains the same definition as before.

The similarity to fixed manufacturing cost effects is obvious given that other variable manufacturing costs affect the same components of current assets. Also, another substantive difference between the target-ROI approach and classical profit maximizing is observable in the foregoing relationship. Note that since $C > 1$, target pricing requires a price increase to exceed an increase in variable manufacturing cost (volume held constant). For our division, $C = 1.3914$. Thus, the price increase is over 39 percent greater than the cost increase.

Although practicing managers will hardly be surprised at this requirement, the result is significant. Almost any approach that assumes profit maximization will predict, or require, price to increase by less than variable cost. Profit-maximizing approaches, for a given level of production, predict reductions in profit when costs increase. On the other hand, the target-ROI approach predicts profit increases with cost increases. Of course, all this presupposes that the firm can increase price by the required amount while holding its volume. Obviously, neither theory is sufficient to explain the behavior of the firm; but the comparison is instructive.

Table 4-2 summarizes the effects of a $1.00 increase in other variable manufacturing costs, $\Delta V' = \$1.00$, on the 40-percent target price, revenue, EBIT, and total assets for the HMD. Whereas price increases that would maintain ROI in the face of increases in fixed manufacturing costs depend on volume, increases in price to offset increases in variable manufacturing costs do not depend on volume in the relation,

$$\Delta P = C \Delta V'.$$

However, the effects on all other components do depend on volume. The relations underlying the numbers in table 4-2 follow.

Table 4-2
Price Effects for an Increase in Other Variable Manufacturing Costs

Initial Volume (Millions)	ΔP	P_2	Δ (Revenue) (Millions)	Δ (EBIT) (Millions)	Δ (Total Assets) (Millions)
2	$1.39	$110.47	$ 2.78	$0.48	$ 1.19
4		64.15	5.57	0.95	2.38
6		48.71	8.35	1.43	3.58
8		40.99	11.13	1.91	4.78
10		36.36	13.91	2.38	5.95
12		33.27	16.70	2.86	7.15
14		31.07	19.48	3.34	8.35
16		29.41	22.26	3.81	9.53
18		28.13	25.05	4.29	10.73
20		27.10	27.83	4.77	11.93

Note: $\Delta V' = \$1.00$.

$$\Delta(\text{Revenue}) = CQ\Delta V',$$

$$\Delta(\text{EBIT}) = Q[C(1 - S) - 1]\Delta V',$$

$$\Delta(\text{Total assets}) = Q[C(S/t_c + 1/t_a) + 1/t_c + 1/t_i]\Delta V',$$

$$\Delta(\text{Funds}) = \Delta(\text{EBIT}) - \Delta(\text{Total assets}).$$

It is imperative that managers responsible for the operations of any firm monitor changes in variable costs and take them into account. This is particularly true with respect to the cost of raw materials and purchased components (R). Here again, the target-ROI approach provides valuable guidance. When the cost of raw materials increases by a factor of ΔR, the necessary increase in price, volume held constant, is a straightforward relationship.

$$\Delta P = (\text{Constant})\Delta R.$$

The constant is quite similar to C, differing only by the return required on the increased value of raw-materials inventory. For ease of presentation, let us denote this constant by C_R. Its definition is

$$\text{Constant} = C_R = \frac{1 + K(1/t_c + 1/t_i + 1/t_r)}{1 - S - K(S/t_c + 1/t_a)}.$$

Thus, the target-ROI price must be increased by a greater amount when the cost of raw materials increases than when other variable manufacturing costs increase. The difference, of course, is the need to earn the target return on the increased raw materials inventory.

Table 4–3 summarizes the effects of a $1.00 increase in the cost per unit of raw materials and purchased components, $\Delta R = \$1.00$, on the 40-percent target price, revenue, EBIT, and total assets for the division. Notice that approximately 148 percent of the raw materials cost increase must be passed through, whereas for other variable manufacturing costs the figure was approximately 139 percent. Obviously, had raw materials turnover been lower, the percentage passed through would have been even greater. (From table 2–1, raw materials turnover is six times per year). The relations for Δ(revenue) and Δ(EBIT) are the same as for other variable manufacturing costs except that C_R replaces C. Because of the effect of ΔR on raw-materials inventory, the relation for total assets is

$$\Delta(\text{Total assets}) = Q[C_R(S/t_c + 1/t_a) + 1/t_c + 1/t_r + 1/t_i]\Delta R.$$

Table 4–3
Price Effects for an Increase in Raw Materials Costs

Initial Volume (Millions)	C_R	ΔP	P_2	Δ(Revenue) (Millions)	Δ (EBIT) (Millions)	Δ (Total Assets) (Millions)
2	1.4760	$1.476	110.55	$ 2.95	$0.63	$ 1.57
4			64.23	5.90	1.25	3.13
6			48.80	8.86	1.88	4.70
8			41.08	11.81	2.51	6.28
10			36.44	14.76	3.14	7.85
12			33.36	17.71	3.76	9.40
14			31.15	20.56	4.39	10.98
16			29.50	23.62	5.02	12.55
18			28.21	26.57	5.65	14.13
20			27.18	29.52	6.27	15.68

Note: ΔR = $1.00.

These relations, together with the data in tables 3–1, 3–2, and 3–3, do indicate certain inflationary tendencies facing an economy characterized by mature industries—assuming that these firms price to meet target ROIs. In general, the more mature the industry, the lower the growth in unit volume and the higher the proportion of variable manufacturing costs to total manufacturing costs. Thus, increases in variable manufacturing costs would be more likely to affect prices, since growth in volume is slow; and the required percentage increases in price are much more significant for high-volume firms, which would also characterize mature industries.

In summary, then, managers facing increases in manufacturing costs must increase prices by considerably more than costs increase just to maintain ROI when volume is held constant. Even if they are successful, they face negative flows of funds in the period of the cost, and the price, increase.

Multiproduct Firms

At this point it is worthwhile to comment on the applicability of the model to multiproduct firms or divisions for which averaging across products is *not* reasonable. The coefficients of change, C and C_R, do not require the assumption of a single-product firm: They apply to any product among the many that a division might make. The manager must identify or estimate the turnovers applicable to the particular product, as well as the variable costs, but this is not an insurmountable difficulty.

Managers can use the ratios C and C_R (for each product) to determine price changes even if they are unwilling to allocate fixed manufacturing costs to individual products or lines (and there are very good reasons for not allocating). These coefficients allow managers to make policy statements about price changes and so provide useful tools for analyzing the relationships between cost changes and target-ROI prices.

It is pertinent here to comment on an attitude that, unfortunately, is too prevalent these days: that businessmen get richer during inflation because they raise prices more than their costs increase. Much of the public seems to think that businesses are per se better off with higher profits, even if they need much higher levels of investment. Many people fail to realize that investors will stop investing unless they are compensated adequately. A simple passing on of a cost increase reduces the compensation of investors. The inventory effect has considerable influence here, unless the firm uses LIFO. (Technically, in fact, the inventory effect will still be significant unless the firm uses LIFO with a periodic inventory system rather than a perpetual system. Even then, some paper profits flow through to the income statement.)

Increases in Selling, General, and Administrative Expenses

The approach to increases in fixed selling, general, and administrative (S,G,&A) expenses (F') and unit variable S,G,&A expenses (U) is similar to that used for manufacturing costs. (Note, however, that selling expenses are often intentionally increased in order to stimulate greater volume. This chapter concentrates on price effects, chapter 5 on volume relationships.) When fixed S,G,&A expenses increase by $\Delta F'$, the required increase in the target-ROI price is the same as that implied by an increase in fixed manufacturing cost, except that increases in S,G,&A expenses have no impact on inventories. In this case,

$$\Delta P = C_{F'} \frac{\Delta F'}{Q},$$

$$C_{F'} = \frac{1 + K/t_c}{1 - S - K(S/t_c + 1/t_a)}.$$

Note that the only difference between C and $C_{F'}$ is the absence of the term K/t_i in the numerator of $C_{F'}$. Thus, $C_{F'}$ is less than C, and the required increase in the target-ROI price for increases in fixed S,G,&A expenses is less than for fixed manufacturing costs.

For the HMD, $C_{F'} = 1.29$. Notice that whereas approximately 139 percent of an increase in fixed manufacturing costs (modified by volume) is passed through to the target price, only 129 percent of an increase in fixed S,G,&A expense is passed through.

Questions may arise regarding the allocation of fixed costs. For instance, some costs of regulatory compliance might be treated as either manufacturing or S,G,&A, depending on both accounting convention and the judgment of the firm's managers. In either case, to the extent that an organization uses the target-ROI approach, the effect of inflation is certainly unpleasant. The pro forma effects of price responses to increases in F' are given by the following relations:

$$\Delta(\text{Revenue}) = C_{F'}\Delta F',$$

$$\Delta(\text{EBIT}) = [C_{F'}(1 - S) - 1]\Delta F',$$

$$\Delta(\text{Total assets}) = [C_{F'}(S/t_c + 1/t_a) + 1/t_c]\Delta F'.$$

The algebraic parallel between unit variable S,G,&A expenses, U, and variable manufacturing costs, V, is similar to that between fixed S,G,&A and fixed manufacturing costs. Suppose that the firm experienced an increase in unit variable selling expenses such as packaging and shipping. The required increase in the target-ROI selling price is given by

$$\Delta P = C_U\Delta U,$$

$$C_U = C_{F'} = \frac{1 + K/t_c}{1 - S - K(S/t_c + 1/t_a)}.$$

Like a change in variable manufacturing costs, a change in unit S,G,&A expenses leads to a change in price that is independent of volume. The effects on revenue, EBIT, total assets, and funds are determined by multiplying those effects shown for fixed S,G,&A by volume and replacing F' by U.

The nature of variable revenue selling expenses, S, makes its change relations somewhat different from those presented for other types of expenses. Suppose that the HMD experiences an increase in these expenses, such as sales commissions, from S_1 to S_2. The new target-ROI price would then be given by the relation

$$P_2 = C_S P_1,$$

$$C_S = \frac{1 - S_1 - K(S_1/t_c + 1/t_a)}{1 - S_2 - K(S_2/t_c + 1/t_a)}.$$

Given our previous articulation of the quantity, $1 - S - K(S/t_c + 1/t_a)$, in target pricing, the foregoing relationship should be fairly obvious because

$$[1 - S_2 - K(S_2/t_c + 1/t_a)]P_2 = [1 - S_1 - K(S_1/t_c + 1/t_a)]P_1.$$

Suppose that our HMD is considering an increase in sales commissions of 4 percentage points, raising S from 11 percent to 15 percent. (Sales commissions need not be 11 percent now but could be lower than 11 percent because there could be other S,G,&A expenses varying with revenue.) Alternatively, the firm could experience an increase in the royalty rate on a licensed product or another change having the same effect.

The managers want to know what price they would have to charge to maintain ROI. In this case, $C_S = 1.0544$, implying that the target-ROI price should be increased 5.44 percent in order to maintain a 40-percent return on investment. The overall effects of this increase in variable revenue selling expenses are summarized in table 4–4. The relations yielding the indicated values in the table are:

$$\Delta(\text{Revenue}) = QP_1(C_S - 1),$$

$$\Delta(\text{EBIT}) = QP_1[C_S(1 - S_2) - (1 - S_1)],$$

$$\Delta(\text{Total assets}) = QP_1[(C_S S_2 - S_1)/t_c + (C_S - 1)/t_a].$$

Table 4–4
Price Effects for an Increase in Variable Revenue Selling Expenses

Initial Volume (Millions)	C_S	P_2	Δ (Revenue) (Millions)	Δ (EBIT) (Millions)	Δ (Total Assets) (Millions)
2	1.0544	$115.01	$11.87	$1.36	$3.40
4		66.17	13.66	1.57	3.92
6		49.89	15.45	1.77	4.43
8		41.75	17.24	1.98	4.94
10		36.87	19.02	2.18	5.46
12		33.61	20.81	2.39	5.97
14		31.29	22.60	2.59	6.48
16		29.54	24.39	2.80	7.00
18		28.19	26.18	3.00	7.51
20		27.10	27.97	3.21	8.02

Note: $\Delta S = 4$ percent.

Although the changes in the target ROI-prices observed in table 4–4 seem rather small relative to the change in variable revenue selling expenses, one should not be deceived. Even though the target-ROI price has increased only 5.44 percent for a 36-percent increase in S (0.04/0.11), the value of C has increased to 1.4671. Thus, any effects on price of subsequent increases in costs will be magnified. For instance, any increase in other variable manufacturing costs must be passed through by 147 percent rather than by 139 percent. We shall see that any policy change that affects C not only has an immediate impact, but also carries through to affect *all* subsequent changes.

The objective of this chapter so far has been to illustrate how a firm must increase its target-ROI price, volume held constant, to maintain ROI in response to increases in various costs, taken one at a time. The methods presented, although primarily illustrative, allow managers quickly to estimate the overall operational effects of short-run decisions or events either beyond or within their control. In this respect, our sequential approach is valuable.

In practice, of course, changes are rarely sequential. Many factors, or all, change simultaneously. Sometimes managers initiate them, sometimes external parties. In these cases, the methods of chapter 3 provide more inclusive approaches to pricing decisions. Moreover, firms rarely have the flexibility to alter prices at will when many costs change, either sequentially or all at once. Periodic reviews of price structures (at least quarterly in the contemporary economic climate) that consider aggregate demand; estimations of competitors' actions; economic conditions; desired market shares; other corporate goals; and, of course, the reliability of cost information are necessary.

Responses to Cost Decreases

As noted earlier, the methods of the previous section are theoretically acceptable for any change in any component of cost. These methods yield the change in price required to maintain ROI. However, they present some obvious practical difficulties when costs decrease. We summarize them in the following questions. (1) What manager would lower price without expecting additional volume (if he does not have to)? Prices typically drop because of other competitive factors. (2) What manager would simply maintain ROI by reducing price commensurate with cost reductions, and then observe reduced total revenue and profit? One possible reason would be that the division had a low target ROI and that the funds released in the first period could find more profitable investment elsewhere. In general, however, few managers of nonregulated firms would follow these prescriptions when costs go down, although most should, of course, when costs go up.

We really have no algebraically elegant suggestions to help the practicing manager out of this dilemma, except to say, "If you don't have to, don't lower your price—increase your return." If that is the case, the methods of chapter 2 provide guidance in investigating the effects on ROI of decreases in costs.

But suppose we take another approach. If our division experienced a reduction in cost, it could lower its price to some extent without reducing EBIT and, since cost reductions for constant volume would lower current assets, raise its ROI. The firm that followed this approach could achieve competitive advantages and still show some short-run growth in its key financial indicator. In addition, managers could develop effective statements of policy, such as: (1) if costs increase, raise your price at least as much as that indicated in the previous section; (2) if costs decrease, lower your price no more than indicated in that which follows.

This approach is remarkably simple. For a reduction in any cost component except variable revenue selling expenses, just replace the change coefficient (C, C_R, $C_{F'}$, or C_U) with the quantity $[1/(1 - S)]$. Thus, for a cost reduction the following "at most" relations would hold:

$$\Delta P = [1/(1 - S)](\Delta F/Q),$$

$$\Delta P = [1/(1 - S)]\Delta V',$$

$$\Delta P = [1/(1 - S)]\Delta R,$$

$$\Delta P = [1/(1 - S)](\Delta F'/Q),$$

$$\Delta P = [1/(1 - S)]\Delta U.$$

Following this approach leaves EBIT constant, with revenue and total assets changing exactly as shown before.

In this case, perhaps one illustration should suffice. Table 4–5 summarizes the effects of this approach given a $1.00 decrease in the cost of raw materials and purchased components ($\Delta R = -\$1.00$). Notice that although approximately 148 percent of an increase is passed through, only about 112 percent of a decrease (again, at most) is passed through. Nevertheless, the firm passes through more than the reduction in cost while maintaining profit and increasing ROI. Also observe that a significant amount of funds is released. This release of funds is even greater than that provided under the methods of the previous section, since EBIT remains constant. (Compare table 4–5 with table 4–3).

For variable revenue selling expenses, similar at-most price reductions require replacing C_S with the quantity $[(1 - S_1)/(1 - S_2)]$.

Table 4-5
At-Most Price Reductions for a Decrease in Raw Materials Costs

Initial Volume (Millions)	$\Delta P = \Delta R [1/(1 - S)]$	P_2	Δ(Total Assets) (Millions)	K_2 (Percent)
2	($1.12)	$107.96	($1.39)	40.2
4		61.64	(2.78)	40.4
6		46.20	(4.17)	40.6
8		38.48	(5.56)	40.8
10		33.85	(6.94)	40.9
12		30.76	(8.33)	41.1
14		28.55	(9.72)	41.2
16		26.90	(11.11)	41.3
18		25.61	(12.50)	41.4
20		24.58	(13.89)	41.5

Note: $\Delta R = \$1.00$.

Changing Prices in Response to Changes in Policy and Competitive Conditions

Whereas the previous section focused on the relationships between cost factors and target-ROI prices, this section concentrates primarily on turnovers. In general, turnovers reflect management policies and are, within limits, controllable. Of course, the nature of banking constraints (cash), the nature of the production process and reliability of suppliers (inventories), and the behavior of competitors and customers (receivables) all have significant impacts. Moreover, taking actions to increase turnovers might have serious undesirable consequences. Nevertheless, firms develop and use policy statements such as, "We try to maintain a one month supply of raw materials." The tasks then become determining how to represent a policy as a turnover and how to relate changes in turnovers to necessary changes in the target price. Obviously, the lower the turnover of a component of current assets, the higher the required price and the higher the required change in price when costs change; the real objective, however, is to understand the sensitivities, so that managers can focus their efforts where they can do the most good.

As opposed to costs (except variable revenue selling expenses), a change in any turnover has both a static and a dynamic effect. A decrease in the turnover of a component of current assets requires an immediate increase in the target-ROI price. But the change coefficients would also change, as noted for S, magnifying the effects of subsequent cost increases. This should be emphasized, since the following section concentrates on static effects.

This section has two parts. The first deals with cash and inventory turnover, the second with accounts receivable turnover and its interaction with variable selling expenses.

Price Changes and Cash and Inventory Turnover

Cash management has improved tremendously over the past two decades, with significant effects. The level of investment in cash can have some impact on the firm's target-ROI price or on ROI. When cash turnover changes by $\Delta t_c = t_{c2} - t_{c1}$, the required change in the target-ROI price is

$$\Delta P = \frac{-K(\text{Initial cash expenditures})}{Qt_{c1}t_{c2}[1 - S - K(S/t_{c2} + 1/t_a)]} \Delta t_c.$$

Table 4–6 shows that the target-ROI price is relatively insensitive to small changes in cash turnover once we get to reasonable balances. (What firm has cash turnover equal to one?) Nevertheless, the difference between the target price at $t_c = 12$ and $t_c = \infty$ (meaning no cash) is almost \$1.00 at the 10-million-unit level. This is significant because many divisions of large firms hold little or no cash. Divisional managers who are not held responsible for cash might drop it from the pricing equation. In that case, the relation would be

$$P = [(Q\bar{V} + F)/Q]C + C_q,$$

$$C = \frac{1 - K/t_i}{1 - S - K/t_a},$$

$$C_q = \frac{U + KR/t_r + [F' + dI + K(mdI/t_i + I)]/Q}{1 - S - K/t_a}.$$

But *somebody* holds cash—presumably the corporation. The corporation must generate a return on cash, just as it must on all other assets. Thus, not holding divisions responsible for cash could result in failure to meet the overall target. (This point parallels the one made in chapter 3 regarding the practice of holding managers responsible only for returns on managed assets.) It is possible for the firm as a whole to earn a target ROI without holding divisions responsible for earning returns on all assets (including corporate assets), by setting the target ROI for divisions sufficiently above the required corporate ROI (appendix 1B discussed this point). Still, it seems that corporate management should hold divisional managers responsible

Table 4–6
Target-ROI Price as a Function of Cash Turnover

Cash Turnover	Unit Volume	
	10 million	18 million
1·	$45.35	$35.37
2	39.94	30.86
3	38.13	29.36
4	37.23	28.61
5	36.69	28.16
6	36.32	27.86
12	35.42	27.11
18	35.12	26.86
24	34.97	26.73
48	34.74	26.54
∞	34.52	26.35

for cash. A recent and often quoted survey reported that 93 percent of major U.S. corporations responding to it evaluated investment center performance using ROI, or both ROI and residual income, and that 63 percent of these firms included cash in the divisions' asset bases.[1]

The relationship between changes in the turnover of raw materials and purchased components and required changes in the target-ROI price is quite similar to that of cash. If the turnover of raw materials changes by $\Delta t_r = t_{r2} - t_{r1}$, then the target-ROI price must change by

$$\Delta P = \frac{-KR}{t_{r1} t_{r2}[1 - S - K(S/t_c + 1/t_a)]} \Delta t_r .$$

Table 4–7 summarizes the required 40-percent target-ROI prices for the HMD, assuming various values of t_r. At lower levels of turnover, the differences in target prices are significant. Moreover, low raw materials turnover, unlike low cash turnover, is not a trivial problem. Industries such as food processing, tobacco, and wine making often have turnovers well below one per year. Since the foregoing relationship is independent of volume, such operating constraints have unpleasant effects on either target prices or ROI.

The possibility of trading off the turnover of raw materials against their cost is certainly an interesting one. One obvious possibility would be to achieve volume discounts on raw materials purchases, thus lowering variable manufacturing cost per unit while reducing turnover. Another would be to buy from a supplier who charges lower prices but is less likely to meet delivery schedules. Using such a supplier would necessitate keeping higher safety stocks, which, again, decreases turnover. We can determine the tradeoff between reduced turnover and required reductions in raw materials

Table 4–7
Target-ROI Price Changes as a Function of Raw Materials
Turnover

Raw Materials Turnover (t_{r2})	Required Change in Target Price (ΔP)
0.5	$6.51
1	2.96
2	1.18
3	0.59
4	0.30
5	0.12
6	0.00
12	(0.30)
18	(0.39)
24	(0.44)
48	(0.52)
∞	(0.59)

cost to maintain ROI and simultaneously increase EBIT without changing either price or volume. Obviously, the same type of reasoning applies to trading higher costs for increased turnover. The relationship appears as follows.

$$\Delta R = \frac{KR_1}{t_{r1}t_{r2}[1 + K(1/t_c + 1/t_{r2} + 1/t_i)]} \Delta t_r.$$

For instance, suppose that our HMD could obtain a discount by doubling its order quantity while halving its frequency. Turnover would drop from six (a two-month supply) to three (a four-month supply). Solving the foregoing expression, we find that $\Delta R = -\$0.195$. Therefore, if the discount were about $0.20 per unit of finished product, reducing the cost from $7.00 per unit to $6.80 per unit, then the decision would be justified on ROI grounds (and certainly on profit grounds).

The effect on target-ROI prices of changes in in-process and finished inventory turnover is also significant—especially when turnover is low. When these turnovers change by $\Delta t_i = t_{i2} - t_{i1}$, the target-ROI price must change by

$$\Delta P = \frac{-K[V + (F + mdI)/Q]}{t_{i1}t_{i2}[1 - S - K(S/t_c + 1/t_a)]} \Delta t_i,$$

which again demonstrates the effect of volume in absorbing the fixed costs of manufacturing. Table 4–8 illustrates this relationship for the HMD at two levels of volume. If operations demand high levels of in-process and finished goods, then the ROI price can change substantially. It is true that the availability of finished product, or the reputation of availability in the mind of the customer, might make such price premiums achievable. If such differentials in price are achievable, together with the firm's acceptance of the impact on first-period funds flow, then the firm can maintain ROI and gain significant increases in EBIT.

Increasing the turnover of in-process and finished goods inventory can have a significant impact on funds flow, although, as noted in appendix 2B, the simple definition of funds flow as Δ(EBIT) $-$ Δ(total assets) is incorrect since production and inventory effects require some time to reach a new equilibrium. Nevertheless, a division may be able to maintain its ROI while releasing large amounts of funds for use by other divisions.

Table 4–9 outlines the 40-percent target-ROI price for our HMD, combining the effects of the two inventory turnovers for the 10-million-unit case. This type of illustration is instructive in demonstrating the combined effects of inventory turnovers on ROI prices.

Price Changes and Promotion Tactics: Accounts
Receivable Turnover and Credit Terms

As instruments of overall marketing and financial policy, credit and collection terms affect the operating and financial results of a firm. Certainly, as noted earlier, the usual objective of these instruments is to stimulate additional unit sales volume rather than to affect product price. The interactions of receivables and credit policy on volume are treated in detail in chapter 5. But price also interacts with receivables and credit policy, particularly when earnings and cash-flow goals are considered in addition to ROI.

We begin this section by observing the required change in the target-ROI price given a change in accounts receivable turnover, just as we did for cash and inventory. Initially, we assume that the firm can affect its accounts receivable turnover through price changes, as opposed to prompt-payment discounts or simply by fiat. Thus, if accounts receivable turnover changes by $\Delta t_a = t_{a2} - t_{a1}$, then the target ROI price must change by

$$\Delta P = \frac{-KP_1}{t_{a1} t_{a2} [1 - S - K(S/t_c + 1/t_{a2}]} \Delta t_a.$$

The relationship between the 40-percent target-ROI price and accounts receivable turnover at the 10-million-unit level for our HMD is illustrated in

Table 4–8
Target-ROI Price as a Function of In-Process and Finished Goods Turnover

In-Process and Finished Goods Turnover	Unit Volume	
	10 million	18 million
0.5	$49.84	$39.05
1	41.58	32.21
2	37.45	28.78
3	36.07	27.64
4	35.38	27.07
5	34.97	26.73
6	34.69	26.50
12	34.01	25.93
18	33.78	25.74
24	33.66	25.65
48	33.49	25.50
∞	33.32	25.36

Table 4–9
Target-ROI Price as a Function of Combined Inventory Turnover

Number of Months' Raw Materials	Number of Months' In-Process and Finished Goods						
	1 ($t_i = 12$)	2 ($t_i = 6$)	3 ($t_i = 4$)	4 ($t_i = 3$)	6 ($t_i = 2$)	12 ($t_i = 1$)	24 ($t_i = 0.5$)
1 ($t_r = 12$)	$33.71	$34.39	$35.08	$35.77	$37.15	$41.28	$49.54
2 ($t_r = 6$)	34.01	34.69	35.38	36.07	37.45	41.58	49.84
3 ($t_r = 4$)	34.31	34.99	35.68	36.37	37.75	41.88	50.14
4 ($t_r = 3$)	34.60	35.28	35.97	36.66	38.04	42.17	50.43
6 ($t_r = 2$)	35.19	35.87	36.56	37.25	38.63	42.76	51.02
12 ($t_r = 1$)	36.97	37.65	38.34	39.03	40.41	44.54	52.80
24 ($t_r = 0.5$)	40.52	41.20	41.89	42.58	43.96	48.09	56.35

Note: Volume = 10 million units.

table 4–10. The relationship, even at 10 million units of output, is instructive. If our division accepted only cash sales, it would have to charge only $31.03 per unit to earn the target ROI. If it allowed its customers fifteen

Table 4-10
Target-ROI Price as a Function of Accounts Receivable Turnover

Days' Sales in Ending Accounts Receivable	Turnover (t_a)	Unit Volume	
		10 million	18 million
0	∞	$31.03	$24.06
15	24	31.63	24.17
30	12	32.24	24.65
45	8	32.88	25.14
60	6	33.55	25.65
90	4	34.97	26.73
120	3	36.51	27.91
150	2.4	38.20	29.20
180	2	40.05	30.61
210	1.714	42.09	32.17
240	1.5	44.35	33.90
270	1.333	46.87	35.82
300	1.2	49.68	37.97
330	1.091	52.85	40.44
360	1	56.46	43.16

days to pay (and assuming that, on the average, customers did pay in fifteen days), then it would have to charge $31.63, an increase of $0.60.

To look at the table another way, the firm currently averages ninety days' sales in accounts receivable ($t_{a1} = 4$); if it could reduce that to sixty days' sales ($t_{a2} = 6$), it would be willing to reduce its price by $1.42, to $33.55. The magnitude of the reduction, from the customer's point of view, can be considered a prompt-payment discount. It translates to a 4-percent discount for payment within sixty days, instead of within ninety days. It is likely that most customers would take advantage of this discount, which works out to a 50-percent ROI for the customer ($1.42/$33.55 × 12). However, our calculations assume that variable revenue selling expenses S are 11 percent of the *net* price, $33.55, not of the gross price, $34.97. The validity of this assumption depends on the particular situation. For instance, one common expense is sales commissions, which are likely to be based on gross sales.

As demonstrated in the previous section, however, adjustments to the target-ROI price given changes in turnover also affect revenue, EBIT, total assets, and funds flow. These changes, which can also be significant, should be investigated as part of the overall evaluative process. When accounts receivable turnover changes, and the target-ROI price is modified using the relationship just outlined, the other effects can be summarized by

$$\Delta(\text{Revenue}) = Q\Delta P,$$

$$\Delta(\text{EBIT}) = Q\Delta P(1 - S),$$

$$\Delta(\text{Total assets}) = \frac{Q\Delta PS}{t_c} + Q\left(\frac{P_2}{t_{a2}} - \frac{P_1}{t_{a1}}\right).$$

Table 4–11 summarizes the incremental effect of moving to successively higher levels of accounts receivable (lower turnovers) at a volume of 10 million units by using the relations previously outlined. For instance, if the firm went from cash sales to fifteen-days' receivables, revenue would increase by $6 million, EBIT would increase by $5.34 million, cash balances and receivables would increase total assets by $13.35 million [note that Δ (EBIT)/Δ (total assets) = 40 percent], and the firm would need $8.01 million in additional funds. Similarly, if the firm went from sixty days' sales in receivables to ninety, it would require $18.96 million in additional funds, assuming target-ROI pricing. Obviously, a division can release funds by moving down the last column in table 4–11. (Again, can another division earn more than this division's target ROI on these funds?)

As has been apparent throughout this chapter, we generally do not favor lowering a product price unless the firm has an exceedingly good reason for doing so. Since 15 August 1971, the date of the imposition of peacetime wage and price controls, quite a few real-world firms have shared this sentiment. Thus, it might be more desirable to adjust variable selling expenses to achieve changes in accounts receivable turnover than to change the target-ROI price.

It might be preferable for the division to consider manipulating prompt-payment discounts in order to achieve changes in accounts receivable turnover, rather than changing the target-ROI price. If a prompt-payment discount, denoted s, is offered, then the manager must consider two receivables turnover figures. For those customers who take the discount, the appropriate turnover figure will depend on the length of the discount period. If we denote this turnover t_{a2} and denote the discount period by n, then $t_{a2} = 360/n$, assuming customers pay on the last day of the discount period. Let us use t_{a1} to denote receivables turnover for those customers who do not take the discount. Then, if we use y to denote the proportion of customers who take the discount, total revenue will be $QP(1 - ys)$, and

$$\text{Receivables} = QP\left[\frac{1 - y}{t_{a1}} + \frac{y(1 - s)}{t_{a2}}\right].$$

Table 4–11
Pro Forma Operating Changes as a Function of Receivables Turnover
(*all dollar amount in millions*)

Days' Sales in Ending Accounts Receivable	Δ(Revenue)	Δ(EBIT)	Δ(Total Assets)	Δ(Funds)
0	—	—	—	—
15	$ 6.00	$ 5.34	$13.35	($ 8.01)
30	6.10	5.43	13.58	(8.15)
45	6.40	5.70	14.25	(8.55)
60	6.70	5.96	14.90	(8.94)
90	14.20	12.64	31.60	(18.96)
120	15.40	13.71	34.28	(20.57)
150	16.90	15.04	37.60	(22.56)
180	18.50	16.47	41.18	(24.71)
210	20.40	18.16	45.40	(27.24)
240	22.60	20.11	50.28	(30.17)
270	25.20	22.43	56.08	(33.65)
300	28.10	25.01	62.53	(37.52)
330	31.70	28.21	70.53	(42.32)
360	35.50	31.60	79.00	(47.40)

Note: Volume of 10 million units.

Thus, the effects on the operating results of the division would be given by

$$\Delta(\text{EBIT}) = -ysQP,$$

$$\Delta(\text{Total assets}) = yQP\left(\frac{1-s}{t_{a2}} - \frac{1}{t_{a1}}\right).$$

This formulation assumes, as is reasonable in most cases, that variable revenue selling expenses, such as commissions, apply to the gross selling price rather than to the net.

With $K = \Delta(\text{EBIT})/\Delta(\text{total assets})$, we see that

$$K = \frac{s}{(1/t_{a1}) - [(1-s)/t_{a2}]},$$

which leads to a surprising conclusion. The proportion (or estimated proportion) of customers taking a prompt-payment discount y is immaterial in determining what discount would maintain the target ROI. Of course, this proportion is quite material in EBIT, total assets, and funds. The prompt-payment discount would be

$$s = \frac{K}{t_{a1}t_{a2}(1 - K/t_{a2})} \Delta t_a.$$

This relation is stated in this manner so that one may compare this with the percentage price change using the price-change relation:

$$-\frac{\Delta P}{P_1} = \frac{K}{t_{a1}t_{a2}[1 - S - K(S/t_c + 1/t_{a2})]} \Delta t_a.$$

Thus, the only superficial difference in these relations is the presence of S, variable revenue selling expenses, in the price relation. This is because of the assumption that S is based on gross price. However, the price relation affects all customers, whereas the discount relation must take into account the proportion taking the discount. In the price relation, therefore, t_{a2} *is* the new receivables turnover, whereas in the discount relation,

$$\text{New receivables turnover} = \frac{1}{[(1 - y)/t_{a1}] + \{[y(1 - s)]/t_{a2}\}}.$$

Suppose the manager of our HMD wanted to reduce receivables from ninety days' sales ($t_{a1} = 4$)—perhaps because corporate management has ordered it. He wants to know what discount to offer so that some customers will pay in sixty days ($t_{a2} = 6$) and still maintain the 40-percent target ROI. In this case, $s = 3.57$ percent (we recall that the price relation required a "discount" of about 4 percent). The remaining issue would be to estimate y, the proportion of customers who would take the discount. As a practical matter, however, what customer would pass up a 3.57 percent discount to pay in sixty days instead of ninety? Thus, the likely estimate for y would be 1. This presents one of the difficulties of relating theory to practice. If all customers had the same cost of capital, then, theoretically, y would be either 0 or 1; that is, they would all take it or they would all refuse it. In this case, if $y = 1$ for the 10-million-volume operating level, then the following comparisons would occur:

	Discount ($s = 3.57$ *percent*)	*Price Reduction*
Δ (EBIT)	$(12.48)	$(12.64)
Δ (Total assets)	(31.22)	(31.60)
Δ (Funds)	18.74	18.96

It must be remembered that this funds release is a one-period result. Subsequent funds flows will be Δ(EBIT) less than before. This again points out why credit terms are typically employed to affect volume. But an analysis such as this is important for a divisional manager who has both cash-flow and ROI objectives, particularly since the discount for our HMD can probably be less than 3.57 percent and still accomplish the same reduction in receivables. The manager may, for instance, begin with a "new receivables turnover" figure and a discount figure lower than in the foregoing example, and work backwards to determine the necessary proportion accepting the discount in order to achieve ROI and funds-flow goals.

Changes in ROI or in the Target ROI

We have presented throughout the viewpoint that the firm has a target ROI that it seeks to achieve or maintain. Of course, managers are always looking for ways to increase ROI, and the change coefficients of chapter 2 (table 2–2) are helpful for that purpose. However, it does seem appropriate to stop here and look at the effects on ROI of various combinations of turnovers of in-process and finished inventories and of accounts receivable. Table 4–12 presents the results, which, although relatively unsurprising, are nonetheless interesting. The table uses the 10-million-unit case, with a price of $34.97 and all other variables held constant.

Low turnovers can damage ROI; increasing them from low levels has rapid benefits. Directing attention at already high turnovers is essentially wasted effort or at least likely to be unproductive. It is interesting that

Table 4–12
Actual ROIs as a Function of Accounts Receivable Turnover and In-Process and Finished Goods Turnover

Receiv-ables Turnover	*In-Process and Finished Goods Turnover*							
	1	*2*	*3*	*4*	*5*	*6*	*8*	*12*
1	17.3	19.7	20.6	21.1	21.4	21.6	21.8	22.1
2	23.2	27.5	29.3	30.4	31.0	31.4	32.0	32.6
3	26.1	31.8	34.2	35.6	36.5	37.1	37.9	38.7
4	27.9	34.4	37.3	38.9	40.0	40.7	41.7	42.7
5	29.1	36.2	39.4	41.3	42.5	43.3	44.4	45.5
6	29.9	37.5	41.0	43.0	44.3	45.2	46.4	47.6
8	31.1	39.3	43.2	45.4	46.8	47.8	49.1	50.5
12	32.3	41.3	45.5	48.0	49.6	50.8	52.3	53.8

Note: 10-million unit volume and price of $34.97. Other variables the same as in table 2–1.

improving one turnover, even from a very low level, while the other remains low, is not nearly as effective as simultaneous, albeit less dramatic improvement. The first row and first column of table 4–12 show this. The results would be much more significant if we combined the inventories of raw materials with in-process and finished goods, which is legitimate as long as we hold volume constant. Reducing raw materials turnover would make the lower ROIs even worse.

Suppose that the firm changes its target ROI. What is the effect on the target price? This relation is given by

$$\Delta P = \frac{(\text{Initial total assets})}{Q[1 - S - K_2(S/t_c + 1/t_a)]} \Delta K.$$

For instance, at the 10-million-unit level, the 40-percent target-ROI price was $34.97, and the initial (pro forma) total assets were $300.54 million (see table 3–4). If the firm were to raise the target ROI for this particular division to 45 percent ($\Delta K = 5$ percent), the required change in the target price would be

$$\Delta P = \frac{\$300.54}{(10)(0.775)} (0.05) = \$1.94,$$

and the new target price would be $36.91.

As a further illustration, we noted in chapter 1 how the target ROI may (or should) change when corporate policies or constraints change. For instance, we saw that a change in the tax rate, other factors constant, gave the following expression.

$$\Delta K = \frac{(K_1 - iD)}{1 - T_2} \Delta T.$$

Let us now suppose that our HMD's 40-percent ROI target incorporated the following policies, goals, and constraints: (1) debt ratio (D) of 30 percent; (2) interest rate (i) of 10 percent; (3) growth rate (G) of 17 percent; (4) earnings retention ratio (E) of 50 percent; and (5) income-tax rate of 45 percent. Table 4–13 shows the effects of various changes in the income-tax rate on the target ROI and the target price, at 10 million units of volume. The impact is substantial. Of course, we would not expect prices to drop as much as indicated if the tax rate decreased (although lowering K would reduce C, dampening subsequent price increases). We would, however, expect the magnitudes of the increases.

Table 4-13
Relationship between Income-Tax Rates and 40-Percent
Target-ROI Price

Income-Tax Rate (T_2) (Percent)	Target ROI (K_2) (Percent)	ΔP	Target Price (P_2)
20	28.4	($ 4.26)	$30.71
25	30.1	(3.66)	31.31
30	32.1	(2.94)	32.03
35	34.3	(2.13)	32.84
40	36.9	(1.17)	33.80
45	40.0	0	34.97
50	43.7	1.43	36.40
55	48.2	3.21	38.18
60	53.9	5.55	40.52
65	61.1	8.63	43.60
70	70.8	13.04	48.01

Note: Volume of 10 million units.

Incremental Pricing

Pricing incremental business is a major problem for many firms. Exports and private branding often provide opportunities to use excess capacity or to break into a new market. Of course, any long-term commitment should be scrutinized carefully because it ties up capacity. And although breaking into new markets can be quite beneficial, managers should still be concerned with the short-term effects of such actions. Intrafirm business is another source, which gets into the sticky problem of transfer pricing. The literature generally states that incremental business is acceptable as long as price exceeds variable cost (and any incremental fixed costs associated with the business). That prescription is not suitable for managers seeking a target ROI.

Let us introduce this topic by assuming that the managers of our HMD are planning for the coming year and are reasonably certain of being able to achieve a sales volume of 10 million units at the price that will yield a 40-percent ROI at this unit volume—$34.97 per unit. Moreover, the managers believe that they could sell additional units through export or private-branding channels, without reducing regular sales. (We consider lost regular sales later.) How should the division price the incremental units in order to maintain its target ROI on total operating results?

The solution is relatively straightforward. The HMD must obtain a price that provides an incremental profit of 40 percent on the incremental investment associated with the sales. Therefore, the HMD could price the incremental units to recover variable costs and provide the target return on those current assets that increase with the incremental sales. Thus, the target-ROI price that the HMD could charge is determined simply by dropping all fixed costs and fixed investment from the basic pricing equation. The coefficient C remains the same as before, whereas the old C_q changes, and we denote the new coefficient C_q'. The incremental target-ROI pricing model would then be

$$P = VC + C_q'$$

$$C = \frac{1 + K(1/t_c + 1/t_i)}{1 - S - K(S/t_c + 1/t_a)} \quad \text{(as before)},$$

$$C_q' = \frac{U(1 + K/t_c) + KR/t_r}{1 - S - K(S/t_c + 1/t_a)}.$$

Notice that the target-ROI price on incremental volume does not depend on the number of units of business, either regular or incremental. Thus, the price on the incremental units would apply to any number that the HMD could generate. The reason is that the incremental investment is all variable with volume or revenue. (Later, we see that we must modify this conclusion if there are incremental fixed costs.)

Perhaps more importantly, the values for determining C and C_q' need not be the ones used to determine the original C and C_q. The manager could set a different target ROI or use different costs and turnovers, should these values be different for the incremental business. If the HMD can, say, obtain more favorable credit terms on the incremental business, then it can lower the price and still achieve the target ROI, or maintain the price and increase ROI. First, let us look at the required price assuming that the terms on the incremental sales are the same as those on normal sales. Then the target-ROI price for any number of additional units would be

$$V = \$10$$

$$C = 1.3914$$

$$C_q' = \$2.53$$

$$P = \$16.44$$

Thus, the HMD would be willing to price its product at only $16.44 for such new channels as exports and private brands while maintaining a price of $34.97 on the regular volume of 10 million units. (If the HMD attempted such price discrimination in other domestic channels, it might run into legal problems. Some foreign competitors face such obstacles in the United States.)

Recall from chapter 3 that target-ROI pricing led to strictly linear effects on revenue, EBIT, and total assets as volume increased and as price on all units declined to maintain the target ROI. The relations illustrated at that time parallel those of incremental pricing. The following relation appeared in chapter 3.

$$\Delta(\text{Revenue}) = (\text{Constant})\Delta Q = \$16.44\Delta Q.$$

For target-ROI pricing on incremental units, we know that volume is irrelevant as long as no new fixed costs arise, so that we can let $\Delta Q = 1$. The incremental price then should equal the change in revenue, $\Delta(\text{revenue})$. This can be shown from the following relation.

$$(\text{Constant}) = \frac{V + U + K[V(1/t_c + 1/t_i) + U/t_c + R/t_r]}{1 - S - K(S/t_c + 1/t_a)} = VC + C_q'.$$

Thus, the incremental revenue should be the same whether or not the additional volume is "incremental." When the units are incremental, the price must be equal to the change in revenue, $16.44 per incremental unit. Further, the effects on EBIT and total assets would be exactly the same as those outlined in chapter 3. There we saw that the following relationship prevails where P refers to the incremental price.

$$\Delta(\text{EBIT}) = [(\text{Constant})(1 - S) - U - V]\Delta Q$$

$$= [P(1 - S) - U - V]\Delta Q.$$

This expression is obvious. For our division, $\Delta(\text{EBIT}) = \$3.13$—exactly the profit earned on each incremental unit at the $16.44 price. The return on incremental sales is about 19 percent ($3.13/$16.44), a good deal more than the standard prescription requires (that is, accept incremental business as long as it yields *any* profit). The standard prescription is valid only if the investment associated with the incremental business disappears by the time the investment base is calculated. It is then valid only for book ROI purposes, not for capital budgeting, as chapter 6 shows. Finally, the effects of incremental business on total assets is as follows.

$$\Delta(\text{Total assets}) = [P(S/t_c + 1/t_a) + V(1/t_c + 1/t_i)$$

$$+ U/t_c + R/t_r]\Delta Q.$$

Incremental Units for Export

Suppose that the HMD has developed an export channel with a reasonable expectation of moving an additional 1 million units in the coming period. However, its managers have estimated that unit variable selling expenses (U) for exports will more than triple to around $5 per unit (say, for higher shipping and import duties) and that variable revenue selling expenses (S) will increase to approximately 15 percent of sales (say, for higher commissions to local agents). Further, the credit terms in this new market are net sixty days (yielding $t_a = 6$). The HMD still desires a 40-percent return on investment, so the target-ROI price on these incremental units should be

$$C = \frac{1 + K(1/t_c + 1/t_i)}{1 - S - K(S/t_c + 1/t_a)} = 1.4045,$$

$$C'_q = \frac{U(1 + K/t_c) + KR/t_r}{1 - S - K(S/t_c + 1/t_a)} = \$7.11,$$

$$P = VC + C'_q = \$21.15,$$

assuming, reasonably, no changes in variable manufacturing costs, cash turnover, or inventory turnover.

Table 4–14 presents the pro forma operating results of the HMD for both the initial case and the incremental units, as well as their combined figures. The $21.15 target price yields the target ROI on incremental assets, thereby maintaining the overall target ROI. The flexibility of the target-ROI model in dealing with such matters is limited only by the imagination of the user. For instance, suppose that this new channel required some additional fixed selling expenses (flat payments to sales representatives, for example) that were directly attributable to that new market. Then the term $F'(1 + K/t_c)/Q$ would be added to the numerator of the C'_q equation. Since new fixed costs are now involved, volume becomes an important pricing consideration even for incremental units. Again, note the difference between analyses that focus on profit and the target-ROI approach. Looking only at profit, a manager would simply divide the change in fixed costs by the number of units involved, failing to consider the impact on required cash balances.

Incremental Units for Private Branding

The qualitative issues involved in whether or not to use private branding are as complex as the overall pricing decision itself and are outside the objec-

Table 4–14
Effects of Incremental Pricing for Exports on Pro Forma Results
(millions)

Income Statement	Initial Output (10 million units)	Incremental (1 million units)	Total (11 million units
Sales	$349.68	$21.15	$370.83
Cost of sales			
Variable	100.00	10.00	110.00
Fixed	50.00	0	50.00
Depreciation	12.80	0	12.80
Gross profit	$186.88	$11.15	$198.03
S,G,&A			
Unit variable	15.00	5.00	20.00
Revenue variable	38.46	3.17	41.63
Fixed	10.00	0	10.00
Depreciation	3.20	0	3.20
EBIT	$120.22	$ 2.98	$123.20
Assets			
Current assets			
Cash	$ 8.89	$ 0.76	$ 9.65
Accounts receivable	87.42	3.52	90.64
Raw materials	11.67	1.17	12.84
Other inventory	32.56	2.00	34.56
	$140.54	$7.45	$147.99
Property, plant, equipment	160.00	0	160.00
Total assets	$300.54	$ 7.45	$307.99
ROI	40%	40%	40%

tives of this book. Our interest at this point is in the application of incremental pricing to relatively common situations.

Earlier, we showed that if all costs and turnovers remained the same, the incremental 40-percent target-ROI price for our HMD would be $16.44. Suppose a large retail firm approached our division with the offer to buy up to 1 million additional units at variable manufacturing cost plus 25 percent, or $12.50. (Such offers are not unknown among chain stores.) Purely on the basis of ROI, should our division accept the offer? As things stand now, the answer is obviously no. The methods of this chapter, however, allow us to respond quickly to this offer with some provisions of our own. For illustration, we consider the possibilities one at a time. Suppose that we first ask for payment in ten days. We have already demonstrated that

$$\Delta P = \frac{-KP_1}{t_{a1}t_{a2}[1 - S - K(S/t_c + 1/t_{a2})]} \Delta t_a.$$

With a ten-day payment period, $t_a = 36$, so that

$$\Delta P = -\$1.67 \quad \text{and} \quad P_2 = \$14.77.$$

We still would not accept the $12.50 offer. But, further, suppose that we could reduce variable revenue selling expenses on these incremental units through the elimination of sales commissions, and so forth, and that we estimate the new figure at about 2 percent. Then,

$$P_2 = C_S P_1 = \frac{1 - S_1 - K(S_1/t_c + 1/t_a)}{1 - S_2 - K(S_2/t_c + 1/t_a)} P_1$$

$$= 0.9055 \,(\$14.77)$$

$$= \$13.37.$$

We still are not ready to accept the $12.50 offer. Finally, suppose that we could reduce unit variable selling expenses because of, say, the reduction in transportation charges to as little as $0.65 per unit instead of the $1.50 per unit applicable to regular sales. Then,

$$\Delta P = C_U \Delta U = \frac{1 + K/t_c}{1 - S - K(S/t_c + 1/t_a)} \Delta U = -\$0.89.$$

Now our 40-percent target incremental price is $P_2 = \$12.48$. If our new estimates are valid, we could accept (just barely) the $12.50 offer. The parameters determining our incremental price would then be:

$$t_c = 24$$

$$t_a = 36$$

$$t_r = 6$$

$$t_i = 5$$

$$S = 0.02$$

$$V = \$10$$

$$R = \$7$$

$$U = \$.65$$

$$K = 40 \text{ percent}$$

so that $P = VC + C_q = \$10(1.1323) + \$1.16 = \$12.48$. We could then easily construct pro forma operating statements like those in table 4–14 to account for the effects of these incremental units.

Lost Regular Sales

In practice, private branding might result in losing sales at the regular price as the final customers become aware that "brand X" is really a name brand. The application of the target-ROI approach here depends on the available information and the point of view. For example, the manager might have a firm price for the incremental units and wish to see how many units at the regular price he could lose without reducing overall ROI below the target. Or he might have a good idea how many units he would lose and wish to determine the minimum acceptable price for the private branding.

To illustrate the determination of the allowable number of lost units, we use a combination of the techniques just discussed and the change coefficients from chapter 2. Let us first suppose that the HMD is operating at the 10-million-unit level and has a special order for 500,000 units (0.5 million) at $22, with all other values remaining constant. This is a quite acceptable incremental price, since the 40-percent target price is $16.44. The order would generate additional operating profit of:

$$(EBIT) = Q[P(1 - S) - U - V] = 0.5[\$22(0.89) - \$11.5] = \$4.04$$

and additional investment of

$$(\text{Total assets}) = Q[(PS + U + V)/t_c + P/t_a + R/t_r + V/t_i] = \$9.25,$$

so that the incremental ROI would be 43.7 percent. From table 4–14, we see that the pro forma figures for the 10-million volume are an EBIT of $120.22 million and an investment of $300.54 million, based on a 40-percent target-ROI price of $34.97. Thus, if no original volume is lost, the revised operating results would be

$$EBIT = \$124.26 \text{ million,}$$

$$\text{Total assets} = \$309.79.$$

Now, if we define ΔQ as the number of units, at the regular price, lost to the private brand, the effects on EBIT and total assets (from table 2–2) would be

$$\Delta(\text{EBIT}) = \$19.62\ \Delta Q,$$

$$\Delta(\text{Total assets}) = \$12.55\ \Delta Q.$$

Since the HMD does not want its overall ROI to be less than the target 40 percent, the allowable lost sales units, ΔQ, may be determined by solving the following equation.

$$K = 0.40 = \frac{\text{EBIT} - \Delta(\text{EBIT})}{\text{Total assets} - \Delta(\text{Total assets})} = \frac{124.26 - 19.62\Delta Q}{309.79 - 12.55\Delta Q}.$$

In this case $\Delta Q = 0.0233$ million, so that the HMD could not lose more than 23,300 original units to the private brand and still maintain its target ROI. The manager would then have to decide whether or not that drop is likely.

Transfer Pricing

Transfer pricing concerns many managers of divisionalized firms. The analyses of incremental pricing bear on this subject and provide some interesting insights if we assume that intrafirm business is essentially incremental, so that the selling division does not rely on it for a large proportion of its revenue (if it does, it probably should not be an investment center).

The best transfer price, when the selling division can operate at full capacity selling to outsiders, is market price. However, if the selling division cannot operate at capacity, then the best transfer price—*from the standpoint of the firm*—is incremental cost. (Economists analyzing this problem call it *marginal cost*.) The reason is that, from the standpoint of the firm, decisions on internal transfers are usually make-or-buy decisions, and the relevant costs for those decisions are incremental costs. From another viewpoint, the decision is whether or not to make the final product that uses the transferred item. In either case, if the manager of the buying division is to act optimally, he should be charged the amount that it costs the firm to produce the transferred goods. As might be expected, this viewpoint is unpopular with managers of selling divisions.

A point often overlooked is that the economist's definition of marginal cost quite correctly includes a return to capital. It is not just variable cost plus any incremental fixed costs associated with the business. In practice, however, selling divisions often receive a price that includes allocated fixed costs. In fact, firms often use a full cost basis to set transfer prices in the absence of a competitive market price. Allocating existing fixed costs is an unwise practice and would only coincidentally approximate incremental cost (including return to capital). Our analysis of incremental business shows that a minimum price should provide the target ROI, and that position seems generally appropriate in transfer pricing. In effect, the manager of a selling division would, under our approach, earn the target return on incremental business.

Note that our approach would not allow the manager to recover a portion of fixed costs or to earn a return on them. The only return allowed is on the variable (incremental) investment. In fact, on intrafirm business, there are no receivables and payables from the standpoint of the firm. One division's receivable is the other's payable, and they cancel out in consolidation. It would therefore be wise to drop the receivable term and to require immediate "payment" by the buying division, so that the selling division is not burdened with the additional "receivables."

Another point is that the return allowed on intrafirm business might differ from the one used for planning. The "best" allowable return, again from the standpoint of the firm, is the opportunity cost of capital, which might be higher or lower than the target return used for planning. In fact, the return should, after tax, be at least as high as the cost of capital. Chapter 6 treats this point in more detail.

What we advocate, then, is that intrafirm transfers be priced at variable cost plus a return on the increased investment. (Incremental fixed costs, if any, should also be included, both as costs and, if appropriate, in investment.) The firm should exclude receivables in determining the incremental investment and should not charge the division with earning a return on them.

The basic policy results in the buying division paying a "true" incremental cost, assuming that the ROI used reasonably reflects the opportunity cost of capital. It therefore fosters goal congruence and seems reasonable with respect to maintaining divisional autonomy. Obviously, the foregoing is a superficial treatment of a very complex subject and requires modification in some circumstances. Nonetheless, we think it worthwhile to present the analysis because the subject is important and the model provides a reasonable guide for transfer-pricing policy.

Summary

Setting target-ROI prices is one thing, and changing them in the face of changes in other variables (like costs and turnovers) is another. The use of change relationships, instead of re-solving the basic model, helps managers to see and understand the ripple effects that accompany a simple change, working its way through income and investment and perhaps affecting as many as four types of investment.

Clearly, managers are not alwáys able to change prices in response to changes in other variables; but a knowledge of the required change is valuable, at least as a "best-case" situation. Moreover, an understanding of changes and of change coefficients should enable managers to develop statements of policy: "For each $1.00 increase in materials cost, we must increase selling price by $1.48 to keep up our ROI."

The topic of incremental pricing is important for many firms and is made simpler by the basic ROI model, which considers factors not normally made explicit in other techniques.

Note

1. J.T. Reece and W.R. Cool, "Measuring Investment Center Performance," *Harvard Business Review,* May–June 1978.

5 Target-ROI Volume Tactics

The objective of this chapter is to provide analytical frameworks, similar to those presented in chapter 4, that managers can use to evaluate the volume requirements implied by various courses of action or uncontrollable events, such as cost changes. We will continue to employ target-ROI reasoning since, particularly where volume is concerned, this approach provides a good overall control criterion for operational decisions.

We will find, however, that as long as the target ROI is to be maintained, any spending stimulus to increase unit sales is expensive. Thus, the other goals of the firm also become important—as do the returns available to other divisions of the firm.

We first consider the question of increasing volume, with and without target-ROI pricing, especially with respect to the cost (expressed as investment requirements) of pursuing volume. We then move to analyses of the relationships among changes in volume and changes in manufacturing costs. We follow this with an analysis of growth objectives, the target ROI, and volume requirements. Finally, we outline the important implications of various promotion tactics on target-ROI volume.

The Cost of Increasing Volume: PIMS versus SKIMS

Increasing the unit sales of a product line is a general preoccupation of most managers in U.S. business. But although growth in unit sales is a worthy goal, it may be quite expensive when the price mechanism is employed. The fact that additional unit-sales volume may be costly, however, is certainly no reason to avoid competition. In the contemporary vernacular, the target-ROI approach provides a useful analytical method for, shall we say, PIMS (Profit Impact of Market Strategies) versus SKIMS (Skimming the Market). Advocates of the PIMS, or high-volume strategy, have argued that market share is the prime determinant of the long-term ROI of the firm.[1]

Certainly, the firm with the largest market share has the most degrees of freedom and should have the lowest unit manufacturing cost. If the firm can achieve high unit volume and maintain its short-run ROI as prescribed by our approach, then our recommendation is quite straightforward: Do it. On the other hand, the SKIMS strategy certainly has a role in the overall portfolio approach to strategic planning. Here again, target-ROI thinking proves to be quite valuable. Thus, we begin this section with an analytical method for assessing the "net cost" of increasing volume so that the manager can understand its consequences and, more importantly, the relationship of target-ROI pricing and increasing volume.

In chapter 2 we noted that when volume changes by $\Delta Q = Q_2 - Q_1$, the net effect on operating profit and total assets is given by

$$\Delta(\text{EBIT}) = [P(1 - S) - U - V]\Delta Q,$$

$$\Delta(\text{Total assets}) = \left(\frac{PS + U + V}{t_c} + \frac{P}{t_a} + \frac{R}{t_r} + \frac{V}{t_i}\right)\Delta Q,$$

where price remains constant. Thus, since we have defined

$$\Delta(\text{Funds}) = \Delta(\text{EBIT}) - \Delta(\text{Total assets}),$$

we can realistically say, in the short run, that $\Delta(\text{funds})$ is a measure of the net cost of increasing unit volume. If $\Delta(\text{funds})$ is greater than zero, then there is a "net gain" to the division. Given the foregoing relationships, this would occur if

$$P(1 - S) - U - V > \frac{PS + U + V}{t_c} + \frac{P}{t_a} + \frac{R}{t_r} + \frac{V}{t_i}.$$

Using this inequality to determine the price necessary to produce a net gain from an increase in volume, we can say that

$$P > \frac{V(1 + 1/t_c + 1/t_i) + U(1 + 1/t_c) + R/t_r}{1 - S - S/t_c - 1/t_a}.$$

At first glance, this would seem like a fairly simple requirement for the HMD first illustrated in table 2–1. This inequality requires that price be greater than about $23.84. Since the 40-percent target-ROI price for the division is greater than $23.84 for most levels of volume illustrated, we might be tempted to say that increases in volume show a net positive funds flow.

Unfortunately, this is not necessarily the case. The reason is, of course, that the target-ROI price is decreasing over *all* units of sales with increases in volume. Moreover, given the requirements outlined here, the target-ROI price is decreasing significantly. In chapter 3, assuming target-ROI pricing, we observed that when volume changes by $\Delta Q = Q_2 - Q_1$, the net effect on operating profit and total assets is given by

$$\Delta(\text{EBIT}) = [\text{Constant } (1 - S) - U - V]\Delta Q,$$

$$\Delta(\text{Total assets}) = \left(\frac{(\text{Constant})S + U + V}{t_c} + \frac{\text{Constant}}{t_a} + \frac{R}{t_r} + \frac{V}{t_i}\right)\Delta Q,$$

$$\text{Constant} = \frac{V(1 + K/t_c + K/t_i) + U(1 + K/t_c) + KR/t_r}{1 - S - K(S/t_c + 1/t_a)}.$$

In chapter 4 we noted that the "constant" in fact was the same as the incremental target-ROI price, since total revenue must increase by this amount for each additional unit of sales in order to maintain ROI. For the HMD, this "constant" is $16.44, which yields a Δ(funds) of − $4.70 for each unit of output.

Since the algebraic representation of our target-ROI constant and the price inequality that yields a positive funds flow differ only by the presence of K, the target ROI, the following observation should be obvious: *When target-ROI pricing is employed, increases in volume will yield a net short-run gain in funds flow only if the target ROI exceeds 100 percent.* More specifically, we can say that as long as the change in revenue per unit is less than

$$\frac{V(1 + 1/t_c + 1/t_i) + U(1 + 1/t_c) + R/t_r}{1 - S - S/t_c - 1/t_a},$$

there will be a short-run net cost of achieving increased volume.

But why require additional volume to have a short-run net funds-flow gain? The real requirement for the firm is to be able to earn a reasonable return on increases in current assets that vary with volume. Thus, we have been saying all along that as long as

$$\frac{\Delta(\text{EBIT})}{\Delta(\text{Total assets})} \geq K,$$

then the change is desirable. Moreover, once a certain volume has been reached, growth in unit volume may be readily achievable without offsetting reductions in price. This reasoning can be reinforced by returning to table 3-1, where we see that the lower the volume, the greater the price reduction that will maintain ROI at a higher volume. Thus, it may be necessary to reduce price as indicated to get the HMD up to, say, 10 million units; but further price reductions would not be expected to yield the desired result in volume. But if our division has acquired market dominance at 10 million units, then it might expect normal increases in aggregate demand without any change in price (that is, market share is ensured).

Nevertheless, the manager might still feel that further increases in market share or aggregate demand are desirable but that the price mechanism is not likely to yield the necessary results.

Volume Requirements and Changes in Manufacturing Costs

The change coefficients illustrated in chapter 4 for target-ROI pricing are quite similar to those for target-ROI volume. Let us begin to demonstrate this similarity by developing the relationship between target-ROI volume and changes in fixed manufacturing costs. When fixed manufacturing costs change by $\Delta F = F_2 - F_1$, the change in volume necessary to maintain the target ROI is given by

$$\Delta Q = \frac{1 + K(1/t_c + 1/t_i)}{P(1 - S) - U - V - K[(PS + U + V)/t_c + P/t_a + R/t_r + V/t_i]} \Delta F.$$

In chapter 3 we noted that the denominator of the foregoing equation would appear any time a change in volume is required to maintain ROI. We labeled this term the *volume-change coefficient*. A change in volume, with price constant, must cover all variable costs in addition to providing the target return on all elements of current assets that vary with volume. (In our formulation, all current assets change with changes in volume.) Additionally, this incremental volume must cover the change in fixed manufacturing costs and provide the target return on the increases in cash and inventory that accompany the changes.

Some rather significant implications in the foregoing equation might not be immediately apparent. An inspection of table 5–1 reveals some of them. The table shows the necessary increases in volume given a 10-percent increase in fixed manufacturing costs ($5 million). First, note that as long as the division was initially achieving exactly its target ROI (40 percent), *then the required percentage increase in volume is independent of the initial volume*. Thus, the increase in target-ROI volume for our firm is 3.76 percent per 10-percent increase in fixed manufacturing costs, regardless of its current volume. We have said throughout that the change coefficients of the target-ROI approach enable managers to develop straightforward statements of policy or of required responses to changes. That is, "What must we do to maintain ROI?" Here, the manager can say that the firm requires increases in volume of 0.376 percent for each 1-percent increase in fixed manufacturing costs (3.76 percent for 10 percent).

Second, increased volume is a very effective method for meeting increases in fixed manufacturing costs because the required change is apt to be relatively small. Suppose, for instance, that this $5 million was for increased quality control. Would the higher quality lead to an increase in volume of at least 3.76 percent? Or, to use a different example, if fixed costs are increas-

Table 5–1
Volume Effects as a Function of Changes in Fixed Manufacturing Costs

Initial Volume (Millions)	Target-ROI Price	Incremental Volume (ΔQ) (Millions)	Percentage Increase
2	$109.08	0.075	3.76
4	62.76	0.150	
6	47.32	0.225	
8	39.60	0.300	
10	34.97	0.375	
12	31.88	0.451	
14	29.67	0.526	
16	28.02	0.601	
18	26.73	0.676	
20	25.70	0.751	

Note: ΔF = $5 million.

ing by 10 percent annually, an increase in unit volume of only 3.76 percent is sufficient to absorb this increase and maintain ROI without raising price. Again, remember that we are dealing with changes one at a time, which is rarely the way that they happen. Even so, analyzing multiple changes simply requires a sequential application of each relevant change coefficient, or re-solving with the changed values. It is because we think it important to isolate the effects of specific changes that we deal with them one at a time.

Third, the pro forma effects of the target-ROI responses to an increase in fixed manufacturing cost may be summarized as

$$\Delta(\text{Revenue}) = C_F \Delta F,$$

$$\Delta(\text{EBIT}) = (C_F[P(1 - S) - U - V] - 1)\Delta F,$$

$$\Delta(\text{Total assets}) = \left(C_F\left(\frac{PS + U + V}{t_c} + \frac{P}{t_a} + \frac{R}{t_r} + \frac{V}{t_i}\right)\right.$$
$$\left. + \frac{1}{t_c} + \frac{1}{t_i}\right)\Delta F,$$

$$C_F = \frac{1 + K(1/t_c + 1/t_i)}{P(1 - S) - U - V - K[(PS + U + V)/t_c + P/t_a + R/t_r + V/t_i]}.$$

Although volume increases may be effective in meeting increases in fixed manufacturing costs, they do not necessarily work well when variable manufacturing costs increase—particularly when initial output is high. When variable manufacturing costs other than materials increase by $\Delta V' = V_2' - V_1'$, the increase in volume required to maintain ROI is:

$$\Delta Q = \frac{Q_1[1 + K(1/t_c + 1/t_i)]}{P(1-S) - U - V_2 - K[(PS + U + V_2)/t_c + P/t_a + R/t_r + V_2/t_i]} \Delta V'.$$

Here, raw materials and purchased components remain constant, and, as before, $V = V' + R$. Table 5–2 outlines this relationship for the HMD, again given that it was initially meeting the target ROI (40 percent) and that "other" variable manufacturing costs increase by \$1 (meaning that total unit variable manufacturing costs increase by 10 percent). Tables 5–1 and 5–2 are not comparable because the increase in total variable manufacturing costs is the same as the increase in fixed manufacturing costs, only at a volume of 5 million units. Still, the percentage increases in volume necessary to maintain ROI are quite large in relation to the 10-percent increase in unit variable cost when initial volume is high.

Table 5–2 also indicates that certain kinds of strategies might work poorly under certain conditions. For instance, one source of the increase in cost could be an incentive plan for labor. If the firm is a low-volume producer that is currently constrained by labor shortages, then the necessary ROI-maintaining increases in volume would probably be readily achievable. However, if the firm is a high-volume producer, it would require enormous increases in unit sales to maintain ROI. Of course, managers contemplating such an incentive system would not consider it unless they were very confident of selling the additional units. An incentive system could be an alternative to hiring additional employees. Or the increase in cost could be for overtime premium, which might well be cheaper than hiring. In any case, there is no reason to increase costs if it is not necessary or desirable because of increased output.

Changes in the cost of raw materials and purchased components induce changes in volume similar to, but more pronounced than, those associated with other variable manufacturing costs. The reason, of course, it that materials show up in two inventories, not just one, and the firm needs to earn a return on both. The relationship is

$$\Delta Q = \frac{Q_1[1 + K(1/t_c + 1/t_i + 1/t_r)]}{P(1-S) - U - V_2 - K[(PS + U + V_2)/t_c + P/t_a + R_2/t_r + V_2/t_i]} \Delta R.$$

This relation is outlined in table 5–3 for the HMD assuming that raw materials and purchased components increase by \$1 (so that total variable manufacturing costs increase by 10 percent). Again, we see that increases in

Table 5–2
Volume Effects as a Function of Changes in Other Variable Manufacturing Costs

Initial Volume (Millions	Target-ROI Price	Incremental Volume (Millions)	Percentage Increase
2	$109.08	0.030	1.52
4	62.76	0.124	3.10
6	47.32	0.283	4.72
8	39.60	0.511	6.39
10	34.97	0.812	8.12
12	31.88	1.189	9.91
14	29.67	1.646	11.75
16	28.02	2.185	13.66
18	26.73	2.815	15.64
20	25.70	3.537	17.69

Note: $\Delta V' = \$1.00$.

Table 5–3
Volume Effects as a Function of Changes in Raw Materials Costs

Initial Volume (Millions)	Target-ROI Price	Incremental Volume (Millions)	Percentage Increase
2	$109.08	0.032	1.62
4	62.76	0.132	3.29
6	47.32	0.301	5.02
8	39.60	0.545	6.81
10	34.97	0.866	8.66
12	31.88	1.269	10.57
14	29.67	1.758	12.56
16	28.02	2.338	14.61
18	26.73	3.015	16.75
20	25.70	3.793	18.96

Note: $\Delta R = \$1.00$.

materials costs require stronger responses than do changes in other variable manufacturing costs, because materials costs are inventoried twice.

Simple as this point is, it is likely to be ignored by managers making decisions of the make-or-buy type. Most of the literature on short-term, easily reversible decisions stresses the effects on profits and ignores .the effects on investment. (We will deal with the make-or-buy decision in chapter 6.)

Tables 5-1, 5-2, and 5-3 reinforce the observation made in chapter 4 with respect to the effects of cost increases on the inflationary tendencies in mature industries. We noted in chapter 4 that when volume is held constant, price increases required to maintain the target ROI of a firm like our HMD must be at or above 140 percent of variable-manufacturing-cost increases. Mature industries are generally characterized by high unit volume, slow growth in unit volume, and a high ratio of total variable manufacturing costs to total manufacturing costs. Now we see that the increases in unit volume necessary to maintain the target ROI and to hold price constant when variable manufacturing costs increase are most severe for the high-volume firm. Since this type of growth in unit volume is generally unlikely for mature firms, the inflationary pressure must be enormous. A large number of U.S. industries can only be characterized as mature *with respect to domestic markets*. Certainly, a stimulus to growth to hold down domestic inflationary pressures is through exports (and, of course, new growth industries). Knowledge of the incremental pricing methods of chapter 4 would be instrumental in stimulating such growth. It is evident that certain foreign organizations have understood these points for quite some time.

Changes in the Target-ROI and Volume Requirements

The relationship between volume and the target ROI is important for any manager. Corporate managers might change the target ROI for any number of reasons, and operating managers will be concerned with the implied changes in their operations and the actions that they could take to achieve the new target.

In chapter 1 we showed how changes in specific goals or constraints each would lead to a change in the target ROI. Earnings growth, debt ratio, retention ratio, and the others all should affect the target ROI. Subsequently, we have illustrated various ways in which output is related to the target ROI. We now look at the question of increasing volume requirements that accompany increases in the target ROI. When the target ROI changes, as the result of changes in one or more goals or constraints, by $\Delta K = K_2 - K_1$, the required change in volume is

$$\Delta Q = \frac{\text{(Initial total assets)}}{P(1 - S) - U - V - K_2[(PS + U + V)/t_c + P/t_a + R/t_r + V/t_i]}\Delta K.$$

This relation is illustrated in figure 5-1, the basis for which is an initial

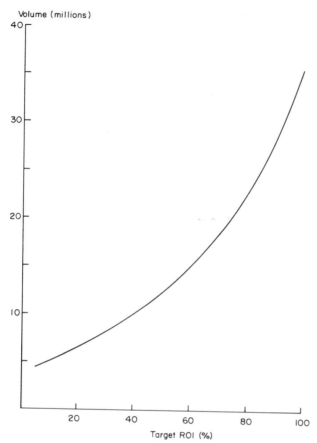

Figure 5-1. Relationship between Target Volume and Target ROI

volume of 10 million units. Further, the relationship between the target ROI and the growth target was demonstrated in figure 1-2.

Let us illustrate this relationship by assuming that the 40-percent target ROI reflected a growth goal (*G*) of 17 percent, a debt ratio (*D*) of 30 percent, a tax rate (*T*) of 45 percent, an earnings retention ratio (*E*) of 50 percent, and an interest rate of 10 percent. Then table 5-4 illustrates how the target ROI and required volume must change as the firm alters its growth target. The table assumes that the HMD was initially operating at 10 million units. The sensitivities are obvious. For instance, if the firm increases its growth goal from 17 percent to 20 percent, then the target-ROI volume must increase by over 1 million units since the target ROI increases to 45.4 percent.

Table 5–4
Volume Effects as a Function of Changes in Earnings-Growth Targets

Target Growth (Percent)	Target ROI (Percent)	Required Volume (Millions)	
		ΔQ	Q
10	26.1	− 2.555	7.445
11	28.2	− 2.205	7.795
12	30.3	− 1.843	8.157
13	32.3	− 1.486	8.514
14	34.3	− 1.118	8.882
15	36.2	− 0.757	9.243
16	38.1	− 0.385	9.615
17	40.0	0	10.000
18	41.8	0.376	10.376
19	43.6	0.765	10.765
20	45.4	1.165	11.165
21	47.2	1.579	11.579
22	48.9	1.983	11.983
23	50.6	2.400	12.400
24	52.3	2.830	12.830
25	53.9	3.249	13.249

Note: Base volume of 10 million units.

At this point we should reiterate that we are dealing with a single-period model. Growth over time in income and investment might come from increases in volume, price, or a combination of these, along with increases in costs. The dynamic case requires considerable analysis at the divisional level, and our model is essentially concerned with identifying tactics for earning the current-period target ROI. The following section briefly discusses how the single-period model can be employed to plan for growth over time.

Meeting Growth Objectives and ROI

Let us suppose that the HMD is operating at 16 million units and is earning its target ROI of 40 percent in the current period. The target growth rate in earnings is 15 percent, so that the HMD, if it is the primary operating unit, must show that increase in EBIT during the next period. Suppose further that the divisional manager expects all costs to increase by 10 percent, either per unit or in total, except that variable revenue selling expenses will remain at 11 percent of sales. Additionally, he expects fixed investment, I, to increase by 10 percent and depreciation expense to do likewise.

In planning for the coming period, the manager would like to know what he must accomplish to meet both the ROI target and the growth target. A variety of results will enable the division to meet, or exceed, one target, but only one price-volume combination will enable it to meet both targets exactly. The manager probably does not expect to hit both targets right on the nose; he would surely be pleased to exceed one while meeting the other. Nevertheless, the price-volume combination that will just meet both targets is certainly of interest because it establishes benchmarks for both price and volume.

Table 5-5 shows the new target values and the calculation of the required price-volume combination. Essentially, the calculation requires the use of the relationship developed in chapter 3 that shows the change in income resulting from changing volume and pricing to meet the target ROI at the new volume.

$$\Delta(\text{EBIT}) = [\text{Constant}(1 - S) - V - U)] \, \Delta Q.$$

We first solve for the required target price at an arbitrary level of volume, calculate the profit at that level, and determine the difference

Table 5-5
Example of Price-Volume Combination to Meet Growth and ROI Goals

Planning assumptions
1. All costs, except S, increase 10 percent over those in table 2-1.
2. Investment and depreciation increase 10 percent.
3. Current year's results: $Q = 16$ million, $P = \$28.02$, EBIT $= \$139.01$ million.

Specific goals
1. EBIT growth of 15 percent. Thus, EBIT $= \$159.85$.
2. Maintain 40-percent target ROI.

First iteration
1. Let $Q_1 = 17.6$ (arbitrary). Then $C = 1.3914$, $C_q = \$10.011$, $P = \$29.664$.
2. EBIT $= \$158.42$.
3. $\Delta(\text{EBIT}) = \$159.85 - \$158.42 = \$1.43$.

Second iteration
1. $\Delta(\text{EBIT}) = [\text{Constant}(1 - S) - U - V] \, \Delta Q$.
2. Constant $= \$18.085$, $\Delta Q = 0.414$, $Q_2 = Q_1 + \Delta Q = 18.04$.
3. $C_q = \$9.845$, $P_2 = \$29.40$, EBIT$_2 = \$159.85$.

between that profit and the one needed to achieve the target growth rate. Because profit in the current period is $139.0 million, achieving the 15-percent increase requires $159.85 in the next period. The table shows that at 17.6 million units, which is the arbitrary level we picked (a 10-percent increase), and a corresponding target-ROI price of $29.66, profit is $158.42 million. Thus, we need an increase of $1.43 million ($159.85 − $158.42). Substituting this increase into the foregoing equation gives a change in volume of 0.42 million, for a volume of about 18.0 million and a new target-ROI price of $29.40. (We should point out that actual income (assuming FIFO) will be higher than this figure by about $5.7 million because of the inventory effects. The model results are, from appendix 2A, based on current-period costs, ignoring the paper profits yielded by FIFO and weighted average.

The increase in volume is about 12.6 percent over the current period, with a price increase of only about 5 percent. These values are the ones that will achieve both targets simultaneously; it might be possible to do better, or impossible to achieve either one or the other or both targets.

Figure 5–2 graphs the familiar price-volume curve that yields the target ROI for the next period. It also shows a price-volume curve that yields the target profit of $159.85. The curves intersect at a volume of 18.02 million and a price of $29.40. The curves illustrate an extremely important difference between planning for profit and planning for ROI. The profit curve lies above the ROI curve until they intersect, then drops below it. As stated in chapter 3, any price-volume combination yields *some* ROI, positive or negative. When the profit curve lies above the ROI curve, the HMD meets the target growth rate and exceeds the target ROI. The meaning is clear: Managers who reduce ROI in order to meet growth targets may be engaging in self-defeating behavior. Because the corporation must expand its asset base faster than it increases its net income, it must do something to sustain the growth rate at the lower ROI. It can increase its earnings retention ratio (which might require increasing equity through external equity financing), it can increase its debt ratio, or a combination of both.

Neither of these alternatives is free of risk. Increasing the retention ratio reduces the current growth rate in dividends per share, which, it is arguable, is as important to investors as is the growth rate in total income or in earnings per share. Chapter 1 pointed to this possibility as one reason that corporate managers must pay attention to the interactions of different growth rates with other key variables.

Increasing the debt ratio is likely to carry along with it an increase in the interest rate and an increase in the return on equity that investors would demand, perhaps resulting in a reduction in the price-earnings ratio. Of course, an increase in the interest rate would also increase the required ROI, although the net effect of an increase in the debt ratio and an increase in the

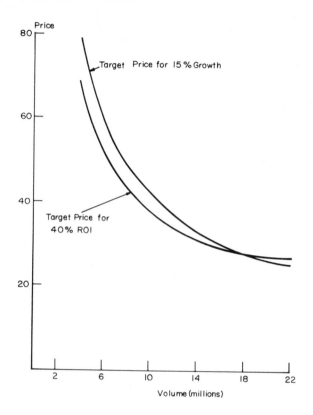

Figure 5-2. Price-Volume Relationship to Meet Growth and ROI Targets

interest rate could still lower the target ROI. This reinforces the point that ROI is the driving force behind corporate profitability and growth and that although financing decisions might enhance, or hinder, the prospects of taking full advantage of ROI in achieving growth, they cannot overcome the effects of a relatively low ROI.

Policy and Promotion Tactics

There is a wide variety of ways to stimulate increased volume, other than the price mechanism. Managers can manipulate many policy variables, such as credit terms, finished goods inventory levels, and various fixed or variable selling expenses, with an eye to increasing unit sales. This section investigates some of these techniques, using the target-ROI-maintaining framework or, equivalently, treating the results as sensitivity analyses showing how much or how little volume must change if we change a policy. As noted earlier, we are of course aware that a manager should be quite willing to forego short-term ROI in order to gain longer-term benefits through either increased demand or increased market share. Nevertheless, we will still adhere to the ROI criterion because of its unifying simplicity and because a manager acting on the basis of other considerations should still understand the implications of the actions for ROI.

Inventory Levels and Volume Requirements

A firm that intentionally increases its level of finished goods inventory (thus lowering its turnover) many times does so with the expectation of increasing unit sales by having more goods available for sale, an expectation that might or might not come true. (It is bound to in some situations, although not necessarily enough to hold ROI.) The method of target-ROI thinking allows the manager to analyze the tradeoff in order to see how much additional volume he must obtain if he reduces turnover. Financial management will be especially concerned with the cash requirements associated with the changes. When the turnover of in-process and finished goods inventory changes by $\Delta t_i = t_{i2} - t_{i1}$, the required change in volume is given by

$$\Delta Q = \frac{K(Q_1 V + F + mdI)}{P(1 - S) - U - V - K[(PS + U + V)/t_c + P/t_a + R/t_r + V/t_{i2}]} \left(\frac{\Delta t_i}{t_{i1}t_{i2}} \right)$$

This relationship, like the corresponding one relating turnover to price (chapter 4), can yield some significant changes—depending, of course, on the magnitude of the change and the current level of volume. For instance, if our division were operating at 10 million units and reduced inventory turnover only from five times per year (a 2.4-month supply) to four times (a 3-month supply), it would need to sell an additional 226,000 units to maintain ROI. Although operating income would increase, so would asset requirements, yielding a negative funds flow. Conversely, if the division were to increase its turnover from five to six times per year, it could give up 147,000 units of sales and still maintain ROI. The question, then, is whether the reduction in inventory would cause volume to drop by that amount. If volume would be unaffected—let us say because the increased turnover is due to better control, and is (unrealistically) costless—then the new ROI would be calculated using the change coefficients from table 2-2.

$$K_2 = \frac{\text{EBIT}}{\text{(Initial total assets)} - \Delta\text{(Total assets)}} \ .$$

Table 5-6 demonstrates how initial volume affects the ROI-maintaining output when inventory turnover is only slightly reduced, from five times (2.4-month supply) to four times (3-month supply) per year. Again, the greater the initial volume, the greater the percentage increase required to maintain the target ROI. As noted in appendix 2A, the effect on funds flow will not be defined by Δ(EBIT) $-$ Δ(total assets) in the short run, since when turnover changes, production will not equal sales until a new equilibrium is reached. Thus, in the short run, inventory is not correctly stated by the relations in 2-2.

Selling Expenses and Volume Requirements

As noted in chapter 4, managers typically manipulate selling expenses with the intention of affecting unit sales volume rather than price. Suppose a manager is contemplating increasing promotion or advertising expenditures. The manager would like to know what incremental volume this expenditure must generate in order at least to maintain ROI; additionally,

Table 5-6
Effects of Initial Volume on Required Output Changes as a Function of a Reduction in Inventory Turnover

Initial Volume (Millions)	Target-ROI Price	ΔQ (Millions)	Percentage Change	Δ(EBIT) (Millions)	Δ(Total assets) (Millions)
2	$109.08	0.023	1.14	$1.97	$ 4.92
2	62.76	0.057	1.42	2.53	6.32
6	47.32	0.102	1.70	3.12	7.81
8	39.60	0.158	1.98	3.75	9.38
10	34.97	0.226	2.26	4.43	11.09
12	31.88	0.305	2.55	5.15	12.87
14	29.67	0.397	2.83	5.92	14.79
16	28.02	0.499	3.12	6.71	16.76
18	26.73	0.614	3.41	7.55	18.86
20	25.70	0.741	3.70	8.43	21.07

Note: $K = 40$ percent, $t_{i1} = 5$, $t_{i2} = 4$.

corporate financial management would want to know the funds requirements for this promotion.

Technically speaking, the relationship between unit sales volume and fixed selling expenses is very similar to that for fixed manufacturing cost. When fixed S,G,&A expenses change by $\Delta F' = F_2' - F_1'$, the required change in volume needed to maintain the target ROI is given by

$$\Delta Q = \frac{1 + K/t_c}{P(1 - S) - U - V - K[(PS + U + V)/t_c + P/t_a + R/t_r + V/t_i]} \Delta F'.$$

This formula is exactly the same as that for fixed manufacturing costs except that $\Delta F'$ does not affect in-process and finished inventory and therefore no return, represented by K/t_i, is required. The relationship between fixed manufacturing costs and target-ROI volume is especially interesting because the promotional change in volume required to maintain the target ROI is independent of initial volume. This is also true of fixed S,G,&A expenses and allows us to articulate a policy statement: "Don't increase fixed promotional expenses unless the expected increase in volume exceeds X percent." For our HMD, each 10-percent increase in fixed S,G,&A expenses requires a 0.70-percent increase in volume.

If we define $\Delta Q = C_{F'} \Delta F'$, where $C_{F'}$ is defined in the preceding equation, we may easily address the question of the investment in promotion, (that is, the total incremental spending associated with it). This amount includes not only the actual expenditure, $\Delta F'$, but also the required increase in external funding, Δ(funds), needed to finance the current assets required to support the new level of activity. The relationships are as follows.

$$\Delta(\text{Revenue}) = PC_{F'}\Delta F',$$

$$\Delta(\text{EBIT}) = (C_{F'}[P(1 - S) - U - V] - 1)\Delta F',$$

$$\Delta(\text{Total assets}) = \left(C_{F'}\left(\frac{PS + U + V}{t_c} + \frac{P}{t_a} + \frac{R}{t_r} + \frac{V}{t_i}\right) + \frac{1}{t_c}\right)\Delta F'.$$

Table 5-7 illustrates the cost of an additional $1 million of promotion—if our HMD is successful in generating the necessary incremental volume. Since the cost of promotion, $\Delta F'$, is included in Δ(EBIT), the investment in promotion for a firm that is successful in generating the necessary incremental volume is simply given by Δ(funds). Notice that Δ(funds) is less than $\Delta F'$ if the firm is successful. For the case in which the firm generates no incremental volume, the cost of promotion is greater than $\Delta F'$ since the additional spending requires the firm to increase its cash balances. In this case, the cost of promotion would be $\Delta F'(1 + 1/t_c)$. For divisions that are

Table 5–7
Target-ROI Volume Effects as a Function of an Increase in Fixed Selling Expenses
(*volume and dollar amounts in millions*)

			Incremental Results for $\Delta F' = \$1$ Million			
Initial Volume	*Volume*	*Percentage Increase*	*Revenue*	*EBIT*	*Total Assets*	*Funds*
2	0.014	1.70	$1.519	$0.192	$0.479	($0.287)
4	0.028		1.748	0.235	0.588	(0.353)
6	0.042		1.977	0.279	0.697	(0.418)
8	0.056		2.206	0.323	0.806	(0.483)
10	0.070		2.434	0.366	0.915	(0.549)
12	0.084		2.664	0.410	1.024	(0.614)
14	0.098		2.893	0.453	1.134	(0.681)
16	0.111		3.121	0.497	1.242	(0.745)
18	0.125		3.351	0.541	1.352	(0.811)
20	0.139	↓	3.580	0.584	1.461	(0.877)

allocated cash on a basis that does not consider S,G,&A disbursement, or not at all, the cost is simply $\Delta F'$.

Because the investment in promotion can be less than the actual change in S,G,&A, there can be a significant leverage effect in promotion. The enterprising divisional manager can use this leverage effect when competing for corporate funds, as can the entrepreneur in leveraging borrowed funds. For instance, suppose that the manager of the HMD wants additional corporate funds for promotion purposes. He believes that he can obtain $5 million from headquarters if he can show an impressive return on the funds—and, of course, he can still maintain the target ROI on total assets. He also knows, from looking at the leverage effect, that the actual budgeted amount for promotion can exceed $5 million—if he is successful in generating the incremental volume.

The manager could then proceed to develop his proposal, as follows. First, if we define Δ(funds) as $5 million, then the manager could budget additional promotional funds by applying the following formula

$$\Delta F' = \frac{\Delta (Funds)}{1 + \dfrac{1}{t_c} + C_{F'}\left(\dfrac{PS + U + V}{t_c} + \dfrac{P}{t_a} + \dfrac{R}{t_r} + \dfrac{V}{t_i} + U + V - P(1 - S)\right)},$$

where $C_{F'}$ is defined as before given the firm's initial volume. Next, the incremental volume necessary to maintain the overall ROI is also defined as before.

$$\Delta Q = C_{F'}\Delta F'.$$

Let us illustrate these relationships for our HMD, working with an initial volume of 10 million units. When Δ(funds) is \$5 million, $\Delta F'$ can be \$9.15 million. This is a significant leverage effect. The incremental volume required to maintain the 40-percent target ROI would then be 641,000 units, a 6.4-percent increase. If this \$9-million promotion effort generated that many additional units, then the incremental operating results would be

$$\Delta(\text{EBIT}) = \$3.33 \text{ million.}$$

Thus, the incremental operating profit yields a return of

$$\frac{\Delta(\text{EBIT})}{\Delta(\text{Funds})} = 66.7 \text{ percent}$$

on the corporate funds. Since Δ(total assets) will be equal to \$8.335 million, the 40-percent target ROI on total operating assets is maintained. (Now all the manager has to do is get the 641,000 additional units!)

Table 5–8 reinforces this leverage effect at various levels of initial volume for our division. The table assumes a \$5-million infusion of funds. Further, it assumes that all available funds that can be budgeted for additional promotion are used. Of course, the table also assumes achievement of the required incremental volume. (In interpreting these figures, however, recall that these data represent a move from one equilibrium point to another. The short-term inventory effect on operating income caused by increased production is ignored. Again, the effect is small.) It can be seen that the leverage effect on available promotional funds is extremely large for the firm with low initial volume (more accurately, with very high proportions of fixed costs and fixed investment to their respective totals); with a target-ROI price of \$109.08 for the 2-million-unit case, it should be. Finally, since the target ROI is being maintained, the return on the \$5 million in external funds is shown to be the same for any level of initial volume. It has to be, since

$$\Delta(\text{Funds}) = \Delta(\text{EBIT}) - \Delta(\text{Total assets});$$

and, therefore, since a return of K is required on total assets, the change in total assets and operating profit is the same for all levels of volume since Δ(funds) is the same. Thus, the change in operating income is simply

$$\Delta(\text{EBIT}) = \frac{\Delta(\text{funds})}{1/K - 1}$$

Table 5-8
Leverage Effect for Promotion Given by an Increase in External Funds

Initial Volume (Millions)	Money Potential for Promotion (Millions)	Required Incremental Volume (Millions)	Percentage Increase in Volume	Percentage Return on External Funds
2	$17.646	0.247	12.4	66.7
4	14.321	0.401	10.0	
6	12.050	0.506	8.4	
8	10.401	0.582	7.3	
10	9.150	0.641	6.4	
12	8.166	0.686	5.7	
14	7.370	0.722	5.2	
16	6.707	0.747	4.7	
18	6.159	0.770	4.3	
20	5.701	0.792	4.0	

Note: Δ(Funds) = $5 million.

(we have reversed the sign in the formula since Δ(funds) is negative), and the change in total assets is

$$\Delta \text{ (Total assets)} = \frac{\Delta(\text{EBIT})}{K}.$$

Before proceding to the next topic, we should say that we are quite aware that the impact of promotion may have significant lag effects and that our period-to-period target-ROI approach is too static to take that fact into account. Nevertheless, we are offering the manager a method of analysis that is useful in evaluating the implications of strategic alternatives; and we certainly do not minimize the importance of this model in formulating such alternatives. Lagged effects would change the values that the manager would use in the following periods for price, volume, or whatever else the promotion was expected to affect. Of special interest in strategic planning is the cost of alternative actions designed to increase market share (see the PIMS reports cited previously). Our approach provides a considerable amount of guidance in assessing costs, including, of course, the investment requirements associated with specific actions. As mentioned in the preface, the model provides a way to spot poorly conceived proposals that focus on incomplete measures of success such as return on sales or income.

Manipulating variable selling expenses to increase unit-sales volume is also an available alternative. Although the leverage effect of variable selling expenses is less than that of fixed selling expenses, the risk involved is also less because some of the increase in total variable expenses comes about only if volume rises (this is a bit rough, as a later section shows). Variable selling expenses in the target-ROI model may be either unit-based (U) or revenue-based (S). We begin our illustrations with unit variable expenses.

Unit Selling Expenses. In the mid-1970s the rebate became a popular method of stimulating unit volume. Let us assume that the HMD is considering a $1.00 rebate $(\Delta U = \$1.00)$ on its product in the hope of gaining additional sales volume. How much additional volume will it need in order to maintain its target ROI (40 percent), and what would be the net cost of the program considering any required external funding? First, when unit variable selling expenses change by $\Delta U = U_2 - U_1$, the change in sales volume required to maintain ROI is given by

$$\Delta Q = \frac{Q_1(1 + K/t_c)}{P(1 - S) - U_2 - V - K[(PS + U_2 + V)/t_c + P/t_a + R/t_r + V/t_i]}\Delta U.$$

Table 5–9 illustrates this relation as well as the pro forma figures that would result if the rebate program achieved the desired results. The table outlines a pattern similar to that of variable manufacturing cost. However, the interpretation of the table can be somewhat deceptive because of the wide range of initial output. It may seem, from the table, that a rebate program has a much greater probability of success at a low initial volume than at a high initial volume. That is hardly the case, however, because a $1.00 rebate at a $100.00 price is not comparable to one at a $20.00 price. Most likely, one would have to be in the higher-volume/lower-price ranges before a $1.00 rebate would have any significance to the consumer. Still, the table again illustrates the high cost of achieving an increase in volume, even when successful. The relations for the pro forma results are given by

$$\Delta(\text{EBIT}) = [P(1 - S) - U_2 - V]\Delta Q - Q_1\Delta U,$$

$$\Delta(\text{Total assets}) = \left(\frac{PS + U_2 + V}{t_c} + \frac{P}{t_a} + \frac{R}{t_r} + \frac{V}{t_i}\right)\Delta Q + \frac{Q_1\Delta U}{t_c}$$

Any analytical approach to management should encourage the evaluation of alternative paths to the same goal. Especially with respect to stimulating volume, the target-ROI method leads the manager to ask some very appropriate questions. For instance, suppose the HMD is currently operating at a volume of 16 million units and is meeting its target ROI, but would like to increase that volume by 10 percent $(\Delta Q = 1.6$ million units) while maintaining ROI. The manager believes that the stimulus must come from promotion.

Table 5-9

Volume Effects and Pro Forma Changes Implied by an Increase in Unit Variable Selling Expenses

Initial Volume (Millions)	ΔQ (Millions)	Percentage Increase	Δ(EBIT) (Millions)	Δ(Total Assets) (Millions)	Δ(Funds) (Millions)
2	0.028	1.4	$0.389	$0.972	($0.583)
4	0.115	2.9	0.968	2.420	(1.452)
6	0.262	4.4	1.746	4.366	(2.620)
8	0.472	5.9	2.732	6.831	(4.099)
10	0.748	7.5	3.935	9.837	(5.902)
12	1.094	9.1	5.365	13.413	(8.048)
14	1.513	10.8	7.035	17.586	(10.551)
16	2.006	12.5	8.949	22.372	(13.423)
18	2.580	14.3	11.129	27.822	(16.693)
20	3.237	16.2	13.581	33.952	(20.371)

Note: $\Delta U = \$1.00$.

Assume that the division can use either a fixed promotion stimulus ($\Delta F'$), such as advertising, or a unit-variable stimulus (ΔU), such as a dealer rebate or some combination of the two. The questions then become, first, how much stimulus is required under each alternative while maintaining ROI (which the model answers); and, second, given the magnitude of the allowable stimulus, which alternative has the greater probability of success (which the manager must decide).

Evaluating the allowable stimulus for $\Delta F'$ and ΔU necessary to achieve the desired ΔQ is straightforward and is accomplished by resolving the relations given previously for $\Delta F'$ and ΔU instead of ΔQ. In the present example, for $Q_1 = 16$ million, $P = \$28.02$, and $\Delta Q = 1.6$ million, these relations would yield

$\Delta F' = \$14.362$ million, or

$\Delta U = \$0.816$, and for both cases

$\Delta(\text{EBIT}) = \$7.138$ million, and

$\Delta(\text{Funds}) = -\$10.707$ million.

Thus, if the firm raised its fixed selling expenses from the current $10-million level to $24.362 million, it would maintain its 40-percent target ROI if it could sell 17.6 million units. Or it could accomplish the same objective by increasing unit variable selling expenses from $1.50 per unit to approximately $2.32. In either case the incremental operating income would be $7.138 million, and the corporate funding requirement would be $10.707 million. Obviously, with no other information, one can only speculate about which alternative would have the greater probability of success. The answer would depend on such factors as past promotion practices, actions of competitors, timing, media, the number of dealers in the distribution system, and so forth. Certainly, risk and leverage should be taken into account, where risk would favor changing variable cost and leverage would argue for changing fixed costs.

Managers could also evaluate combinations of unit variable selling expenses and fixed selling expenses using the target-ROI method. Here it is appropriate to show how the method lends itself to simple "building-block" equations with respect to change relations. Suppose that our divisional manager felt that neither of the alternatives outlined previously would suffice, but that a combination of dealer rebates, ΔU, and incremental fixed promotion, $\Delta F'$, would be likely to achieve the 1.6-million increment in sales volume. The building-block concept relating ΔQ, ΔU, and $\Delta F'$ could be stated with any of the three change variables as the criterion. Thus, suppose that the HMD felt that a $0.50 dealer rebate was appropriate, $\Delta U = \$0.50$, and wanted to know how much incremental fixed promotion could be budgeted to maintain ROI while achieving the desired increase in unit sales. In this case,

$$\Delta F' = \frac{(P(1 - S) - U_2 - V - K[(PS + U_2 + V)/t_c + P/t_a + R/t_r + V/t_i])\Delta Q}{1 + K/t_c}$$

$$- Q_1 \Delta U$$

Here $\Delta F' = \$5.562$ million, and the manager might believe that a combination of a $0.50 dealer rebate and an incremental fixed promotion budget of $5.562 million is an acceptable alternative. The incremental operating profit, $\Delta(EBIT)$, and initial funds requirement, $\Delta(funds)$, would be the same as for the two more-extreme cases outlined previously.

The building-block concept just articulated extends to any combination of change relations that has been, or will be, presented. A manager is often concerned with multiple changes in strategy—and maintaining ROI—and the change relations covered in this book are additive for evaluating alternatives: They can be applied sequentially. For instance, a combination of a price change, ΔP, and a unit variable selling-expense change, ΔU, can be combined in determining the required target-ROI volume change, ΔQ, simply by referring to the previous change relations for volume-price and volume-unit variable selling expense. Then the relation would be

$$\Delta Q = \frac{Q_1(1 + K/t_c)\Delta U - Q_1[1 - S - K(S/t_c + 1/t_a)]\Delta P}{P_2(1 - S) - U_2 - V - K[(P_2 S + U_2 + V)/t_c + P_2/t_a + R/t_r + V/t_i]}$$

Obviously, one could avoid using many of these change relations by re-solving the basic ROI equation in chapter 2 for whatever variable is of inter-est. We are not trying to make the algebra of return on investment unneces-sarily complicated. Basically, we are suggesting that the change relations provide more-direct methods of evaluation and carry more-definitive impli-cations for two-way (or, as in the foregoing, three-way) policy analyses. Moreover, the change relationships are especially helpful for multiproduct firms or divisions because they are applicable to any product taken separately from others. There is no need to allocate fixed costs (except for incremental fixed selling costs) to individual products. Thus, the analyses here can be made independently of others. It is not even necessary to use the same target-ROI figure.

Of course, no manager should really believe, or say, that managing ROI is easy. The cost-volume-profit and current asset relationships in run-ning a manufacturing firm are, in fact, exceedingly complicated. Simplistic ROI models such as "margin times turnover" or sage advice like "you must earn a return on your accounts receivable" have intuitive appeal but little information content. The target-ROI approach may be algebraically threat-ening, but it does present a reliable method for managers to use in analyzing the overall effects of various classes of decisions on ROI, price, volume, operating profit, and funds flow. To do this, one simply must have equa-tions. The complexity of the change relationships reflects the complexity of the real-world relationships. Changes in one variable lead to changes in others, rippling throughout the elements of profit and investment.

Variable Revenue Expenses. Managers often manipulate variable revenue selling expenses to spur unit volume instead of unit variable selling ex-penses. Commissions, price discounts, and so forth are typically per-dollar, rather than per-unit, amounts. An increase in advertising and promotion budgets based on a percentage of revenue is a typical example. When variable revenue selling expenses change by $\Delta S = S_2 - S_1$, the unit sales volume required to maintain ROI is given by

$$Q_2 = \frac{P(1 - S_1) - U - V - K[(PS_1 + U + V)/t_c + P/t_a + R/t_r + V/t_i]}{P(1 - S_2) - U - V + K[(PS_2 + U + V)/t_c + P/t_a + R/t_r + V/t_i]} Q_1$$

Table 5-10 outlines this relation for the HMD assuming revenue variable selling expenses increase from 11 percent to 15 percent. Notice that table 5-9 and 5-10 both show that the required percentage increase in volume grows as the initial level of volume rises. In discussing table 5-9, we noted that this was deceptive because the probability of stimulating volume by changing unit variable selling expenses is likely to be low at low levels of volume because of the much higher target-ROI prices at low volumes. A

$1.00 rebate does little when the price is $80 or so. The same conclusion does not hold for variable revenue selling expenses because they are a constant percentage of price. Thus, fixed expenses and variable expenses show a consistent and predictable relationship with volume. Changes in fixed expenses require a constant proportional change in volume, regardless of initial volume, to maintain ROI; changes in variable expenses require an increasing proportional change.

This does not necessarily indicate, however, that the use of fixed expenses is preferable for high-volume firms. If incremental volume is desired, then the question is which method, or combination of methods, is most likely to achieve the objective—and how much it will cost. We observed earlier how much fixed selling expenses (F') and/or unit variable selling expenses (U) could be increased to yield 10-percent increase in volume (from 16 million units to 17.6 million units) for the HMD. For variable revenue selling expenses, the relation is

$$S_2 = \frac{(P - U - V - K[(U + V)/t_c + P/t_a + R/t_r + V/t_i]\Delta Q + Q_1 PS_1(1 + K/t_c)}{PQ_2(1 + K/t_c)}$$

For the preceding case,

   $S_2 = 0.139,$

   $\Delta S = 0.029,$

   $\Delta(EBIT) = \$7.138$ million, and

   $\Delta(Funds) = -\$10.707$ million.

Thus, an increase in variable revenue selling expenses from 11 percent to 14 percent will accomplish the same goal (for example, a 10-percent increase in volume while maintaining ROI) as an $0.82 increase in unit variable selling expenses or a $14.362 increase in fixed selling expenses. The manager's knowledge of the marketplace should then be applied to the choice of alternatives, considering both probabilities of success and risk.

These relationships point up a problem with using flexible budget allowances based on revenue. Some firms budget advertising and promotion in this way. The increase in volume required to justify an increase in the percentage allowed could be quite large. Here, a 2.9-percentage-point increase requires a 10-percent increase in volume. Although most writers frown on this type of flexible budget allowance, there is evidence that many firms use it. The point is that, at a minimum, the division should be able to justify any increases on ROI grounds, not just on profit grounds.

Table 5–10
Volume Responses and Pro Forma Results as a Function of a Change in Revenue Variable Selling Expenses

Initial Volume (Millions)	Target-ROI Price	ΔQ (Millions)	Percentage Change	Δ(EBIT) (Millions)	Δ(Funds) (Millions)
2	$109.08	0.129	6.5	$ 1.751	($ 2.626)
4	62.76	0.301	7.5	2.554	(3.831)
6	47.32	0.515	8.6	3.435	(5.153)
8	39.60	0.774	9.7	4.480	(6.720)
10	34.97	1.079	10.8	5.676	(8.515)
12	31.88	1.431	11.9	7.018	(10.528)
14	29.67	1.832	13.1	8.519	(12.778)
16	28.02	2.283	14.3	10.187	(15.280)
18	26.73	2.786	15.5	12.015	(18.022)
20	25.70	3.343	16.7	14.023	(21.035)

Note: $\Delta S = 4$ percent.

Comparison of Methods

We have looked at the three ways of manipulating selling expenses and have commented that increasing fixed expenses is riskier but offers greater potential rewards than does increasing variable expenses. Those comments need some refining. The real question in a risk-return tradeoff of the sort considered here is the commitment associated with each strategy. It is quite likely that the firm would not commit the entire budgeted incremental expense in one shot: It would increase the fixed portion of the promotional budget in steps, thus cutting down the commitment and lessening the risk if early signs failed to give convincing evidence that the plan was working.

Conversely, increasing variable expenses, whether per unit or per dollar, carries the risk that sales volume will not increase. Whether or not it does, the division could wind up with higher variable expenses on the base-level volume. The question then becomes whether or not it could rescind the dealer rebate, higher commission, or other inducement. If not, the division might well be taking more risk by increasing variable expenses than by increasing fixed expenses.

Suppose that we are considering three different strategies for changing selling expenses. All three require the same incremental volume, and thus the total increase in selling expenses must be the same for all changes. That is, the increase in total per-unit or per-dollar expenses must equal the increase in fixed expenses. This should be obvious because all these expenses show up in the same places—on the income statement and as additional cash requirements on the balance sheet. This assumes, of course, that each strategy works exactly as planned and that each gives equal incremental volumes. The question of return is clear: If each of the strategies actually yields more than the required incremental volume, then profits and ROI will be highest under the fixed cost strategy.

On risk, the question of commitment is crucial. Let us consider a single example. We saw earlier that a $14.362-million increase in fixed expenses that provided a 1.6-million increase in volume would maintain ROI, as would an increase of $0.816 in unit selling expenses, if it led to the same increment in volume. If the firm announced a rebate of that amount and then found no perceptible effect on volume, it might be stuck with the rebate for some time. The risk, then, is the $0.816 on the existing 16 million units, which is $13.056 million, only $1.306 less than the $14.362. This analysis suggests that the risk of increasing the fixed costs is not much more than that of increasing the variable costs. Of course, each situation will be different; nevertheless, part of the analysis should be devoted to ascertaining the commitment under each strategy.

Credit Policy and Target-ROI Volume

Managers can use credit policy to affect unit-sales volume. Just as we found for target-ROI pricing in chapter 4, accounts receivable turnover can have a significant impact on the volume required to achieve the target return on investment. When accounts receivable turnover changes by $\Delta t_a = \Delta t_{a2} - \Delta t_{a1}$, the change in volume necessary to maintain the target ROI is given by

$$\Delta Q = \frac{-KQ_1P}{P(1 - S) - U - V - K[(PS + U + V)/t_c + P/t_{a2} + R/t_r + V/t_i]} \left(\frac{\Delta t_a}{t_{a1}t_{a2}} \right)$$

Table 5-11 illustrates this relationship for our firm with an initial volume of 10 million units and a receivables turnover of four. The results could be either exciting or depressing, depending on the sensitivity of sales volume to the payment period. For instance, if the firm extended its payment period so that the day's sales in receivables went from an average of 90 days ($t_{a1} = 4$) to an average of 120 days ($t_{a2} = 3$), it would require an additional 867,000 units to maintain its 40-percent target ROI. If customers

Table 5-11

Relationship between Volume and Accounts Receivable Turnover

Days' Sales in Receivables	t_a	Target-ROI Quantity (Millions)	EBIT (Millions)	Receivables Investment (Millions)
0	∞	8.068	$ 82.322	$ 0
15	24	8.336	87.589	12.147
30	12	8.623	93.219	25.130
45	8	8.931	99.250	39.038
60	6	9.261	105.728	53.975
90	4	10.000	120.223	87.425
120	3	10.867	137.255	126.678
150	2.4	11.900	157.510	173.388
180	2	13.149	182.017	229.902
210	1.714	14.690	212.269	299.644
240	1.5	16.642	250.563	387.971
270	1.333	19.191	300.598	503.354
300	1.2	22.662	368.704	660.410
330	1.091	37.667	466.920	886.900
360	1	35.508	620.781	1,241.709

Note: $P = \$34.97$.

were, on the whole, responsive to such a change, however, operating profit would increase by over \$17 million (a 14-percent increase). And, assuming that the 40-percent target ROI is a higher return than the firm could earn elsewhere, the incremental funds requirement would be a desirable investment. On the other hand, if customers were completely insensitive to the payment period, then the effect on ROI, from table 2-2, would be:

$$K_2 = \frac{\text{EBIT}}{\text{Initial total assets} - (QP\Delta t_a)/t_{a1}t_{a2}} = 36.5 \text{ percent.}$$

Thus, if no incremental units were realized, the drop in ROI would be quite significant, whereas the incremental-funds requirement would be:

$$\Delta(\text{Funds}) = \frac{QP\Delta t_a}{t_{a1}t_{a2}} = -\$29.4 \text{ million.}$$

Although the target-ROI approach offers no help in predicting whether or not a particular change will occur (nor does any other method that we know of), it does permit quantification of the effects of changes and prediction of the results of partial success.

We have spent most of this chapter discussing relationships with respect to increases in volume, but we could just as well have examined decreases. An inspection of table 5-12 gives some idea of the relationship between allowable decreases in volume (for example, those that maintain the target ROI) and policy variables such as accounts receivable turnover.

If the HMD was currently operating at a volume of 10 million units and moved to a strictly cash basis for sales, it would be able to give up 1.932 million units of volume; its operating profit would decrease from \$120.22 million to \$82.31 million, $\Delta(\text{EBIT}) = -\$37.91$ million; but it would release funds in the amount of \$56.87 million to other corporate uses. The throwoff would be less for a division earning, say, 20 percent, but it would still be substantial. Thus, a division of a firm may become a "cash cow" and still maintain the target ROI on those assets it still controls. Of course, this is a one-shot infusion. In subsequent years the division would throw off less cash than it would have if it had kept the higher volume. Once running at equilibrium, the division would throw off cash equal to profit plus depreciation.

Let us reinforce this notion. Suppose that corporate management decides, because of its perception of aggregate demand, growth in demand, market share, and so forth, to place the HMD on a harvest mission, turn it into a cash cow—or whatever contemporary phrase the organization uses. It can maintain its target ROI and still throw off a large amount of funds to other divisions with greater prospects for growth. Table 5-12 outlines how this would work if receivables were eliminated ($t_{a2} = \infty$) for each level of initial volume (target-ROI pricing is still assumed). The results are highly significant, *provided that they are achievable.* Certainly, one would question why a division with a 40-percent ROI would be placed on a harvest mission; but the data are primarily for illustration. One possibility is that the division's assets are old and its ROI reflects low net book values. Also, one might assume that the division might have to change variable selling expenses or institute discounts in order to induce cash sales. This relationship was examined in chapter 4.

Summary

This chapter showed that increasing unit volume through the price mechanism is expensive with respect to funds requirements. Nevertheless, the target-ROI method shows how the firm must increase its volume, through increases in aggregate demand or in market share, in order to maintain ROI.

Table 5-12

Allowable Volume Reductions and Pro Forma Results for the Elimination of Accounts Receivable

(*millions*)

Initial Volume	No Account Receivable ($t_{a2} = \infty$)		
	ΔQ	$\Delta (EBIT)$	$\Delta (Funds)$
2	−0.260	($22.247)	$33.371
4	−0.587	(26.027)	39.041
6	−0.977	(29.901)	44.852
8	−1.426	(33.863)	50.795
10	−1.932	(37.911)	56.867
12	−2.491	(42.035)	63.052
14	−3.101	(46.229)	69.344
16	−3.759	(50.506)	75.759
18	−4.462	(54.840)	82.260
20	−5.209	(59.242)	88.863

Note: $t_{a1} = 4$.

Although increasing unit volume is effective in absorbing increases in fixed costs, it is not very helpful in absorbing increases in variable costs, especially if unit volume is already high. Thus, managers of high-volume firms must be especially careful in controlling variable costs.

The dynamic applications of the target-ROI method demonstrate that when the division has both a target ROI and a target growth rate in EBIT, it can achieve both targets only at a single price-volume combination. The use of tactics related to policy and promotion to stimulate unit volume is also quite expensive and can require substantial commitments and high risk. The target-ROI method allows the manager to assess the magnitudes of commitment and risk—a useful first step in arriving at a decision.

Note

1. For a primary source on the PIMS (Profit Impact of Market Strategies) study, see S. Schoeffler, R.D. Buzzell, and D.F. Heany, "Impact of Strategic Planning on Profit Performance," *Harvard Business Review,* March–April 1974; and R.D. Buzzell, J.G. Bradley, and R.G.M. Dalton, "Market Share—A Key to Profitability," *Harvard Business Review,* January–February 1975.

6

Target ROI and Capital Expenditures

Managers generally acknowledge that the best way to evaluate investment alternatives is to use discounted-cash-flow (DCF) techniques, not book ROI, and we agree. So far in this book we have worked with book ROI as the criterion for investment (and disinvestment) decisions, and we now turn to a reconciliation of book-ROI and DCF methods. (For the sake of brevity, we will refer to investment, rather than to investment and disinvestment.) We begin with an analysis of investments in working capital, which have been the type so far considered; and then move to investments in fixed assets.

It is important to emphasize at the outset that target-ROI methods are in no way substitutes for DCF methods. Target ROI is an operating construct. Book-ROI methods are intended primarily to serve the analytical requirements, of say, the divisional manager held accountable for book ROI. Major capital-budgeting decisions are primarily corporate decisions, and the general manager must use DCF models to analyze and sell his proposals. However, where there is a direct equivalence between DCF and target-ROI methods, as we will demonstrate for investments in working capital, the substitutability is appropriate. The two most widely used discounted-cash-flow models, net present value (NPV) and internal rate of return (IRR), give the same signals as our method—to accept or reject the investment. Even if there is no direct equivalence, as is the case with fixed investment, the manager must still be concerned with the effects of such investments with respect to both meeting future ROI targets and to making the changes (increased price or output, reduced costs, and so forth) required for maintaining the target ROI. Of course, the incompatibility between discounted-cash-flow methods and book ROI for investments in fixed assets is well known and gives rise to some sticky problems in evaluating divisional managers.

Target-ROI Equivalence to DCF for Working-Capital Investment

Chapter 3 developed a set of relations stating the effects of increasing volume on operating profit, total assets, and funds flow when target-ROI pricing is employed. To reiterate, when volume increases by ΔQ, then

$$\Delta(\text{EBIT}) = [\text{Constant}(1 - S) - U - V]\Delta Q,$$

$$\Delta(\text{Total assets}) = \left(\text{Constant}\left(\frac{S}{t_c} + \frac{1}{t_a}\right) + V\left(\frac{1}{t_c} + \frac{1}{t_i}\right)\frac{U}{t_c} + \frac{R}{t_r}\right)\Delta Q,$$

$$\text{Constant} = \frac{U + V + K[V(1/t_c + 1/t_i) + U/t_c + R/t_r]}{1 - S - K(S/t_c + 1/t_a)}.$$

For the HMD, we showed that

Constant = \$16.44 (equivalent to incremental pricing),

$\Delta(\text{EBIT}) = \$3.13\Delta Q$, and

$\Delta(\text{Total assets}) = \$7.83\Delta Q = \Delta(\text{WC})(\text{WC} = \text{working capital})$.

Obviously, the change in total assets is exclusively in current assets or working capital, since no increase in fixed investment is taking place. The specific changes amount to an increase in cash and equivalents equal to [constant $(S/t_c) + (V + U)/t_c] \Delta Q$; an increase in receivables equal to constant $(1/t_a) \Delta Q$; an increase in raw materials and purchased components equal to $(R/t_r) \Delta Q$; and an increase in in-process and finished goods inventory equal to $(V/t_i) \Delta Q$.

In order to relate these target-ROI results to classical capital-budgeting models, it is appropriate to convert the results to an after-tax basis. Thus, the after-tax earnings generated by this incremental output would be

$$\Delta(\text{profit}) = \Delta(\text{EBIT})(1 - T),$$

where, as in chapter 1, T denotes the corporate income-tax rate. Assuming $T = 46$ percent, $\Delta(\text{profit}) = \$1.69 \Delta Q$ for the HMD. Since the investment associated with this incremental profit is working capital, no depreciation is involved; therefore, $\Delta(\text{profit})$ also represents $\Delta(\text{cash flow})$ in capital-budgeting terminology (with the proviso that none of the changes is confounded by product-costing methods, as discussed in the appendix to chapter 2).

A few other assumptions are necessary in order to relate the target-ROI figures to capital-budgeting terminology. First, we must estimate an "expected life" of the incremental cash flows (for the moment, at least). We will use N to denote this estimated life. Second, we will assume that the incremental cash flows occur at the end of the year—a common assumption. Third, since the investment in working capital builds up during the period, as does cash flow, we also assume the investment "occurs" at the end of the first year. Fourth, we assume that investments in working capital are recovered one year after the end of the estimated life of the cash flows. Investments in working capital are usually recoverable, not always in total but usually close enough for us to assume full recovery as a basis for analysis. Thus, for capital-budgeting purposes, the pattern of investment and cash flow would appear as follows.

Cash flow	Δ(Profit)	Δ(Profit)	. . .	Δ(Profit)	Δ(WC)
Investment	Δ(WC)				

Year	0	1	2	. . .	N	N + 1

The discounted-cash-flow method would then yield a net present value (NPV), as given by

$$\text{NVP} = \Delta(\text{Profit}) \sum_{j=1}^{N} (1 + r)^{-j} + \Delta(\text{WC})(1 + r)^{-(N+1)} - \Delta(\text{WC})(1 + r)^{-1},$$

where r is the discount factor employed in the capital-budgeting decision. When the decision maker sets NPV equal to 0 and solves for the value of r that will accomplish this, the resultant r is referred to as the *internal rate of return* (IRR). For the HMD, the IRR would be given by solving the following relation for r.

$$1.69\Delta Q \sum_{j=1}^{N} (1 + r)^{-j} + 7.83\Delta Q(1 + r)^{-(N+1)} - 7.83\Delta Q(1 + r)^{-1} = 0.$$

Regardless of the value of N, the estimated life, the solution to the foregoing equation yields IRR = 27.55 percent. Thus, we see that a pretax, target-ROI criterion of 40 percent on incremental working capital is equivalent to an after-tax internal rate of return of 27.55 percent. We now proceed to demonstrate that the internal rate of return on incremental working capital has a simple and direct relation to the target ROI, regardless of what type of decision yields the increase in working capital (changes in turnover, price changes, and so forth).

It is commonly understood that for nondepreciable investments the reciprocal of the payback period is also the internal rate of return, provided that the annual cash flows are equal and the original investment is returned at the end of the life. Since we are assuming that cash flows accrue at the end of each year and the working capital investment occurs at the end of the first year, the payback period is given by

$$\text{Payback} = \frac{\text{Investment}}{\text{Annual cash flow}} = \frac{\Delta(\text{WC}) - \Delta(\text{Profit})}{\Delta(\text{Profit})}.$$

We know that $\Delta(\text{profit}) = \Delta(\text{EBIT})(1 - T)$ and that, for the firm that employs target-ROI methods, $\Delta(\text{EBIT})/\Delta(\text{WC}) = K$. Therefore,

$$\text{Payback} = \frac{\Delta(\text{WC}) - \Delta(\text{EBIT})(1 - T)}{\Delta(\text{EBIT})(1 - T)} = \frac{1 - K(1 - T)}{K(1 - T)}.$$

The payback period on incremental working capital for a firm with a 46-percent tax rate and a target ROI of 40 percent will then be 3.63 years. The internal rate of return is then

$$\text{IRR} = \frac{1}{\text{Payback}} = \frac{K(1 - T)}{1 - K(1 - T)},$$

which is the definition of IRR initially developed in chapter 1. For the HMD, IRR, according to this formula, is 27.55 percent. *Thus, the equivalence with classical, and computationally tedious, IRR methods using this simple approach is exact.* Moreover, the relationship holds for any estimated life of the increase in EBIT. The result should be quite appealing to a general manager who is attempting to sell a proposal requiring an increase in working capital.

Of course, a manager does not have to be strictly employing *target*-ROI methods to make use of the relationships outlined here. The IRR is related to the ROI on the incremental investment, whether or not that is the target ROI. Obviously, managers will sometimes have opportunities to invest at better, or worse, rates of return. (Accepting an opportunity with an expected ROI below the current level is perfectly appropriate in several circumstances, for example, when residual income is the basis for evaluation.) For instance, the internal rate of return on working capital for incremental volume at a constant price can be quite instructive. Using the equations developed in this chapter and in chapter 2, the IRR on incremental volume would be given by

$$\text{IRR} = \frac{[P(1 - S) - U + V](1 - T)}{(PS + U + V)/t_c + P/t_a + R/t_r + V/t_i - [P(1 - S) - U - V](1 - T)}.$$

Thus, the IRR on working capital predicted by new volume depends heavily on price. Obviously, if the firm employs target-ROI pricing, then this equation reduces to $K(1 - T)/[1 - K(1 - T)]$. If the added volume can be achieved at the current price, the IRR can be quite attractive, which, of course, is to be expected. For the HMD, for instance, a price that exceeds

$43.61 provides an essentially infinite IRR on working capital for additional output.

In this book, we have developed five concepts of a target price. The first is the method discussed in chapter 3 for pricing to achieve a target ROI on *total investment* based on expected output. The other four concepts of target pricing all are related to the pricing of incremental units of output. First, of course, any price on incremental business should exceed ($U + V$)/(1 − S) in order to cover variable cost. This relation follows directly from the material in chapter 2. For the HMD, this amounts to $12.92. Second, in chapter 4 we developed the concept of a target-ROI price on incremental output. For the HMD, the 40-percent target-ROI incremental price amounted to $16.44. Third, in chapter 5 we developed the relation for a price on incremental output that is necessary to provide a positive pretax cash flow; this was shown to be equivalent to the incremental price for a 100-percent target ROI. This price was $23.84 for the HMD. Now we see a fourth incremental price, one that will achieve an essentially infinite IRR on increased working capital. This relation is given by

$$P > \frac{(U + V)(1 - T + 1/t_c) + R/t_r + V/t_i}{(1 - S)(1 - T) - S/t_c - 1/t_a},$$

which is simply requiring that annual, after-tax cash flow exceed incremental working capital. Again, for the HMD, this amounts to $43.61.

In summary, the concept of target-ROI decision making and classical capital-budgeting procedures show a direct equivalence for investments in working capital. This equivalence, although certainly important, should not be overemphasized. This is because the IRR model itself contains some significant deficiencies, principally the assumption that the firm can invest its inflows at the IRR. We now turn to an examination of the target-ROI model as it applies to investments in fixed assets.

We begin by pointing out that we are illustrating methods to determine the responses needed to earn the target ROI in the first year of the new investment. This is a more-stringent requirement than most corporations should impose on divisions. Nevertheless, managers need to look at the effects on book ROI of investments that they make on DCF grounds. Thus, one might wish to examine the relationships that follow in conjunction with the change coefficients from table 2–2, which can be used to determine ROI if the change in price or volume is not enough to yield the target ROI in the first year.

We might also point out that many firms use gross book values in calculating ROI and that this has some advantages over net book value, one of which is that changes in it indicate changes in IRR.[1]

Target-ROI Applications to Fixed Investment

Investment in Distribution Facilities

A simple and appropriate place to begin an analysis of target-ROI applications to fixed investment is in selling and administrative activity. This is because S,G,&A activity (cost or investment) does not directly affect finished and in-process inventory. Moreover, investment in the selling function is typically undertaken to increase sales volume; and incremental output is a common starting place in capital budgeting discussions.

Specifically, then, assume that a divisional manager is considering an investment in new distribution facilities. The target-ROI model allows the manager, along the lines of chapter 5, to develop answers to such questions as: "If we invest ΔI dollars in new distribution facilities, how much additional volume must we generate in order to maintain ROI?" It is appropriate here to recognize that increased fixed investment ordinarily brings increased fixed operating costs that require cash, F'. New distribution facilities require personnel, heat and light, property taxes, and so forth. Analytically, therefore, we will assume that the managers have estimated the ratio of increased cash S,G,&A expenses to fixed investment, $\Delta F'/\Delta I = b$. Thus, with this amendment, we can say that when fixed investment changes by ΔI, the required change in output is given by

$$\Delta Q = \frac{b + d + K(1 + b/t_c)}{P(1 - S) - U - V - K[(PS + U + V)/t_c + P/t_a + R/t_r + V/t_i]}\Delta I.$$

The denominator of this equation is the now familiar volume-change coefficient, the explanation of which would be redundant. The numerator simply states the increases in fixed costs, $(b + d)\Delta I$, that must be covered and the return of K on the change in total assets, $(1 + b/t_c)\Delta I$, that must be provided by the new volume.

Let us illustrate this relation for the HMD. First, since 80 percent of the current end-of-year fixed investment of $160 million is in manufacturing (that is, $m = 0.8$), then $32 million is in administrative and selling activities. Further, let us suppose that $12 million is allocated to administration, so that $20 million is investment in selling (including distribution activities). A 10-percent increase in this amount would be a *beginning*-of-year outlay of $2 million. If we assume the HMD uses straight-line depreciation over a ten-year estimated life, then the end-of-year investment would be $\Delta I = \$1.8$ million. Third, since the depreciation rate, d, is based on end-of-year balances, then $d = 0.111$ the first year. (Notice that $d\Delta I = \$0.2$ million, representing annual depreciation.) Finally, suppose that the managers estimate that fixed cash S,G,&A expenses will increase by 12.5 percent of the increase in investment, so that $b = 0.125$. These conditions allow us to develop the data in table 6–1, which details the incremental volume required to maintain a 40-percent target ROI given a 10-percent ($2-million) increase in fixed investment for distribution. Notice that, as in the fixed-expense sections of chapter 5, a constant percentage increase in unit volume is required for any level of initial volume—assuming that the target ROI was already being achieved. This is extremely useful information with which to develop simple but appropriate statements of investment policy (for example, "for a 10-percent increase in distribution facilities, we require a 0.79-percent increase in unit volume").

The expressions relating changes in fixed investment to changes in operating profit, total assets, and funds flow implied by the target-ROI model are very instructive with respect to classical capital budgeting. If we define $\Delta Q = C_I \Delta I$, where C_I is given in the previous relation, then,

$$\Delta(\text{Revenue}) = PC_I\Delta I,$$

$$\Delta(\text{EBIT}) = (C_I[P(1 - S) - U - V] - b - d)\Delta I,$$

$$\Delta(\text{Total assets}) = \left[1 + \frac{b}{t_c} + C_I\left(\frac{PS + U + V}{t_c} + \frac{P}{t_a} + \frac{R}{t_r} + \frac{V}{t_i}\right)\right]\Delta I,$$

$$\Delta(\text{Funds}) = \Delta(\text{EBIT}) - \Delta(\text{Total assets}).$$

Table 6–1
Incremental Volume Necessary to Maintain a 40-Percent ROI Required by an Increase of 10 Percent in Fixed Investment for Distribution

Initial Volume (Millions)	Target-ROI Price	ΔQ (Millions)	Percentage Increase
2	$109.08	0.016	0.79
4	62.76	0.031	
6	47.32	0.047	
8	39.60	0.063	
10	34.97	0.079	
12	31.88	0.094	
14	29.67	0.110	
16	28.02	0.125	
18	26.73	0.142	
20	25.70	0.157	

Note: $\Delta I = \$1.8$ million.

Assuming an initial output of $Q_1 = 16$ million units, the relations are summarized in table 6-2 for the HMD. The table also presents a detailed verification of Δ (funds) for this particular case. An initial expenditure of $2 million for distribution facilities requires an increase of 125,000 units (from table 6-1) to maintain a 40-percent target ROI. If achieved, this new volume will increase operating profit by $1.126 million, yielding a pretax cash flow of $1.466 million after adding back depreciation. Also, incremental working-capital requirements for cash, accounts receivable, raw materials inventory, and in-process and finished goods inventory of $1.366 million will occur. This figure yields a first year, pretax external-funds requirement of $1.90 million (again ignoring the small inventory effect for increased production before sales and production return to equilibrium).

How does this type of pretax, target-ROI analysis relate to classical capital-budgeting procedures? First, of course, one must convert the pretax cash flow to an after-tax figure. This is given by

$$\Delta(\text{Cash flow}) = \Delta(\text{EBIT})(1 - T) + d\Delta I.$$

Table 6-2
Pro Forma Effects of Incremental Output from Increased Investment in Distribution Facilities

$\Delta Q = C_I \Delta I = 0.0125$

$C_I = 0.070$

$\Delta(\text{EBIT}) = C_I[P(1 - S) - U - V] - b - d \ \Delta I = \$1.266$

$\Delta(\text{Total assets}) = \Delta(\text{EBIT})/K = \$3.166$

$\Delta(\text{Funds}) = \Delta(\text{EBIT}) - \Delta(\text{Total assets}) = -\$1.900$

Statement of Funds

Cash flow			
Δ (EBIT)		$1.266	
Depreciation		0.200	1.466
Investment			
Distribution facilities		$2.000	
Working capital			
Cash	$0.086		
Accounts receivable	0.882		
Raw materials inventory	0.147		
Other inventory	0.251	1.366	3.366
Δ (Funds)			($1.900)

Note: All figures in millions except C_I. Initial volume of 16 million units.

For the example in table 6-2, Δ(cash flow) = $.884 million. Second, we must assume a pattern of cash flows and working-capital flows similar to that discussed earlier in this chapter. Specifically, working investment occurs at the end of the first year and is returned one year after the "termination" or the expected life. Cash flows occur at the end of the year. Assuming, as is typical, that the investment in fixed assets occurs at the beginning of the first year, that the expected life is the depreciation period (ten years), and that there is no salvage value, then the pattern of flows for the data in table 6-2 would appear as follows.

Returns		0.884	0.884	. . .	0.884	1.366
Investment	2.0	1.366				

Year	0	1	2	. . .	10	11

The assumption implicit in this pattern of flows is that, after the first year, stable output, pricing, and costs occur—gradually increasing ROI on end-of-year *book* investment. All these assumptions point out the difficulty of relating target-ROI methods to classical capital budgeting. Nevertheless, if we define r as the internal rate of return on this investment, then r would be given by

$$F(r) = \$0.884 \left(\frac{1 - (1 + r)^{-10}}{r}\right) + \$1.366(1 + r)^{-11}$$
$$- \$1.366 (1 + r)^{-1} - \$2.000.$$

This rather messy relation (which is, however, easy to solve with modern calculators) yields an internal rate of return of r = 26.97 percent. Thus, our target-ROI method, utilizing a 40-percent target for the HMD, results in a quite acceptable investment in IRR terms. Moreover, using the previously derived relation (for investment in working capital) that IRR = $K(1 - T)/[1 - K(1 - T)]$, this same example would show the internal rate of return to be 27.55 percent, a figure not far from the more-exact IRR calculated previously. This comparability of the simple IRR relation with the more-exact relation is quite good until the target ROI becomes large, as illustrated in figure 6-1. This graph plots the IRR from the more-exact formula assuming a price of $28.02 (as was used in tables 6-1 and 6-2 for Q_1 = 16 million) and varies the assumed incremental target ROI from 5 percent to 85 percent. At different prices, the more-exact IRR will change, especially at higher target ROIs.

Nevertheless, the comparability of the two methods is quite good at the levels of K in which most companies operate. We are not suggesting, however, the substitution of the simple IRR equation for the more-exact one by practicing managers when substantive investment decisions are being made. The principal reason is that in the real world there are too many other

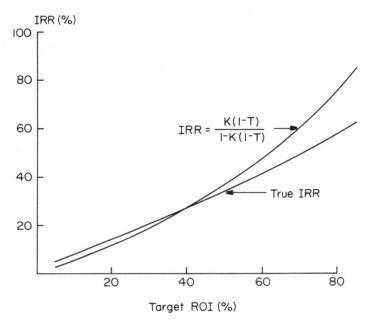

Figure 6-1. Comparison of IRRs, by Estimated and More-Exact
Calculations for Investment in Distribution Facilities Using
Target-ROI Model

important factors, such as investment tax credits, accelerated depreciation, salvage values, and so forth, that must be incorporated into more-exact DCF methods that cannot be handled by the simple method. The illustration was intended primarily to show how the target-ROI method yields good—and quick—information for the manager.

Investments in fixed assets for distribution are often incurred in order to reduce variable selling expenses rather than to increase unit volume. Where unit variable selling costs are concerned, the firm may increase its fixed investment in order to reduce transportation or shipping charges. If the target ROI is to be maintained, an incremental fixed investment of ΔI should yield a reduction in unit variable selling expenses, as given by the relation

$$\Delta U = -\left(\frac{b + d + K(1 + b/t_c)}{1 + K/t_c}\right)\left(\frac{\Delta I}{Q}\right)$$

If such a reduction in unit variable selling expenses can be achieved, and if we redefine $\Delta U = -C_I \Delta I/Q$ (C_I redefined previously), then the pro forma incremental operating figures would be

$$\Delta(\text{EBIT}) = (C_I - b - d)\Delta I,$$

$$\Delta(\text{Total assets}) = [1 - (C_I - b)/t_c]\Delta I.$$

Thus, the first-year increment in total assets (ending balance) would be less than ΔI since a reduction in working capital, in the form of cash balances, is achieved.

The firm may also use the foregoing relation somewhat differently. It may turn the relation around and find out the maximum allowable incremental investment that would both maintain the target ROI and reduce unit variable selling expenses by ΔU. This is illustrated in table 6–3 for the HMD. The table shows the investment necessary to achieve a reduction of $0.50 (from $1.50 to $1.00) in U while maintaining a 40-percent ROI. The assumption that $b = 0.125$ is maintained. Note that, in the second column, the initial, beginning-of-year investment outlay is given by the ending investment plus first-year depreciation. (Initial investment $= \Delta I + d\,\Delta I$, where the ten-year straight-line depreciation schedule is again used; thus, $d = 0.111$.) For instance, if our firm could achieve a $0.50 reduction in unit variable selling expenses at an operating volume of 16 million units, it could invest *up to* $14.160 million in fixed assets. Such a reduction would reduce working-capital requirements (cash) by $267,000 and yield an increase of

Table 6–3
Maximum Fixed Investment Allowed to Reduce Unit Variable Selling Expenses $0.50 per Unit
(Millions)

	Incremental Fixed Investment			
Volume (Q)	End of First Year (ΔI)	Beginning ($\Delta I + d\,\Delta I$)	Reduction in Working Capital $(b - c)\,\Delta I/t_c$	Incremental Operating Profit $(c - b - d)\,\Delta I$
2	$ 1.593	$ 1.770	$0.033	$0.624
4	3.186	3.540	0.067	1.248
6	4.779	5.310	0.100	1.872
8	6.372	7.080	0.133	2.495
10	7.965	8.850	0.167	3.119
12	9.558	10.620	0.200	3.743
14	11.151	12.390	0.234	4.367
16	12.745	14.160	0.267	4.991
18	14.338	15.930	0.300	5.615
20	15.931	17.701	0.334	6.239

almost $5 million in operating profit. As illustrated earlier, DCF methods would look favorably on such a venture, and the next question would be directed toward finding an investment alternative of less than $14 million that would give a similar reduction in U.

A similar approach could be taken with respect to the fixed investment required to reduce variable revenue selling expenses. Many small, growing firms have very large variable revenue selling expenses because they must use various middlemen to sell their product. As they mature, undertaking fixed investment to develop, say, their own retail outlets may become an important decision. Analytically, the choice here is the same as for unit variable selling expenses. If the target ROI is to be maintained, an incremental fixed investment of ΔI should yield a reduction in variable revenue selling expenses, as given by

$$\Delta S = -\left(\frac{b + d + K(1 + b/t_c)}{P(1 + K/t_c)}\right)\left(\frac{\Delta I}{Q}\right).$$

This, of course, implies that $\Delta S = \Delta U/P$, an obvious relation. Thus, all pro forma results would be equivalent to those shown in table 6-3.

Investment in Manufacturing Facilities

Managers invest in manufacturing facilities for many reasons: to increase productive capacity, to improve product quality or reliability, to reduce direct labor or other variable production costs such as raw materials, or possibly to reduce inventory through the purchase of materials-handling equipment.

Let us begin this section with the relation between investment in fixed manufacturing assets and product price. Manufacturing firms do invest in such fixed-asset categories as quality-control equipment, more-reliable processing equipment, and so forth, with an objective of improving unit margins through higher prices or of staving off price reductions. Moreover, the contemporary regulatory environment often requires firms to invest in manufacturing-related facilities that have little, if any, impact on unit volume or production efficiency. Thus, in order to maintain the target ROI, a firm must raise prices. In fact, it is likely that an entire industry would raise prices; consider, for example, statements by representatives of the automobile industry regarding the cost, and price, per car of various regulations.

In order to introduce the price-to-investment relation, we will again assume that increases in fixed costs are linearly related to increases in fixed investment. We will represent increased fixed manufacturing costs as

$\Delta F = a \Delta I$. Thus, an investment in manufacturing facilities of ΔI, if volume is assumed to remain constant, will necessitate a price increase, ΔP, to maintain the target ROI, as given by

$$\Delta P = \left(\frac{a + d + K[a/t_c + (a + d)/t_i + 1]}{1 - S - K(S/t_c + 1/t_a)} \right) \left(\frac{\Delta I}{Q} \right).$$

This relation is illustrated in figure 6-2 for our HMD assuming $a = 0$ (no increase in fixed manufacturing costs) and $a = 0.3$ (a substantial increase), given a 10-percent increase in fixed assets allocated to production. (The 10-percent figure was estimated as follows: Since $m = 0.8$, the initial investment of $160 million amounted to $128 million for manufacturing. Thus, since $12.8 million would be a beginning-of-year 10-percent increase, and assuming a ten-year straight-line depreciation schedule, ΔI would be $11.52.) The relation just shown, as well as the pattern illustrated in figure 6-2, certainly justifies the argument of many low-volume firms that reguulation-inspired investments actually give a competitive benefit to higher-vol-

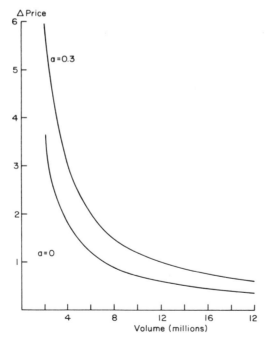

Figure 6-2. Target-Price Increases for Increases of 10 Percent in Fixed Manufacturing Investment

ume firms. And since high-volume firms often have market power, such investments could raise prices.

If we define $\Delta P = C_I \, \Delta I / Q$, the effects on operating results predicted by the foregoing would be

$$\Delta(\text{EBIT}) = [\, C_I(1 - S) - a - d\,]\Delta I,$$

$$\Delta(\text{Total assets}) = \left(\frac{C_I S + a}{t_c} + \frac{C_I}{t_a} + \frac{a + d}{t_i} + 1\right)\Delta I.$$

However, the model definition of Δ(funds) must be modified somewhat because of the fixed-cost effect on in-process and finished goods inventory, both cash costs and depreciation. Thus, the actual free-cash requirement would be given by

$$\Delta(\text{Funds}) = \Delta(\text{EBIT}) - \Delta(\text{Total assets}) + (a + d)\Delta I/t_i$$

$$= [\, C_I(1 - S - S/t_c - 1/t_a) - a(1 + 1/t_c) - (1 + d)\,]\Delta I.$$

Suppose that our HMD must disburse $12.8 million for pollution-control equipment, representing a 10-percent increase in existing fixed manufacturing assets. Further, assume that increases in manufacturing overhead associated with the operation of this equipment will amount to 30 percent of end-of-year incremental investment, setting $a = 0.3$. If the equipment is depreciated over a ten-year period, then $d = 0.111$ in the first year and $\Delta I = \$11.52$. If our HMD was currently operating at a 10-million level of volume, then in order to maintain its 40-percent ROI, it would have to raise its price $1.24, assuming no additional volume. If it was at the target-ROI operating level before the investment, then $P_1 = \$34.97$, and the increase would be 3.55 percent. The pertinent pro forma operating information is outlined in table 6–4. However, if this increase were achievable, the division would also show an increase in operating profit of $6.308 million. This would be offset by a negative first-period funds flow of $8.515 million.

As a brief digression, we consider the overall "social cost" of regulation implied by business firms' seeking to maintain target ROIs. Using our HMD as a frame of reference, we have seen that prices might increase 3.55 percent for the example in table 6–4. But there are other costs, specifically a significant increase in the overall level of taxation. Let us present an extremely conservative estimate of this overall increase.

First, if the HMD borrowed the entire amount of Δ(funds) needed to finance the equipment at, say, a 10-percent interest rate, then taxable income would increase by $5.46 million. At a 46-percent income-tax rate, the incremental taxes would be $2.517 million before an investment tax

Table 6–4

Target-ROI Price Increase and Pro Forma Results Required by a 10-Percent Increase in Fixed Assets Allocated to Manufacturing

$$\Delta P = \frac{a + d + K[a/t_c + (a + d)/t_i + 1] \,\Delta I}{1 - S - K(S/t_c + 1/t_a)} \quad \frac{}{Q} = C_I(\Delta I/Q) = \$1.24$$

$\Delta \text{(EBIT)} = [C_I(1 - S) - a - d]\,\Delta I = \$6.308 \text{ million}^a$

$$\Delta \text{(Total assets)} = \left(\frac{C_I S + a}{t_c} + \frac{C_I}{t_a} + \frac{a + d}{t_i} + 1 \right) \Delta I = \$15.770$$

$\Delta \text{(Funds)} = [C_I(1 - S - S/t_c - 1/t_a) - a(1 + 1/t_c) - (1 + d)]\,\Delta I = \$-8.515$

Statement of Funds

Cash flow			
Δ (EBIT)		$6.308	
Depreciation		1.280	$7.588
Investment			
Pollution-control equipment		$12.800	
Working capital			
Cash [$(C_I S + a)\,\Delta I/t_c$]	$0.201		
Receivables $(C_I S\,\Delta I/t_a)$	3.102	3.303	16.103
Δ (Funds)			($ 8.515)

Note: $\Delta I = \$11.52$ million, $Q = 10$ million, $a = 0.3$, $d = 0.1111$.
^a All figures following in millions.

credit. Assuming a credit of 10 percent on the $12.8 million, the tax bill for our HMD increases by $1.23 million. This leaves $4.23 million as increased earnings after taxes. Assuming a 40-percent payout ratio and a 25-percent marginal tax rate to stockholders (both very low), our equity holders pay increased taxes amounting to $0.42 million. Even worse, suppose further that the HMD sells only to consumers and that the average sales tax rate is 5 percent (both very conservative assumptions). The incremental sales taxes would total $0.62 million. Thus, taxes have increased over $2.27 million, which could pay the salaries of quite a few regulators. If the division were industrial and its customers employed target pricing (remember chapter 4), the overall social cost would rise even more rapidly. It may be that the "social benefit" of this example, in terms of, say, lives saved, would justify this social cost. The point is, however, that it *is* expensive.

As noted in earlier chapters, costs or investments are typically incurred to increase unit-sales volume rather than to increase prices. Thus, the incremental volume required to maintain the target ROI when fixed manufacturing assets increase by ΔI can be found from the following relation.

$$\Delta Q = \frac{a + d + K[a/t_c + (a + d)/t_i + 1]}{P(1 - S) - U - V + K[(PS + U + V)/t_c + P/t_a + R/t_r + V/t_i]} \Delta I.$$

Table 6-5 outlines this relation for various initial volumes and fixed-manu-facturing-cost proportions (that is, values of a). We again note the constant proportional increase in output required to maintain the target ROI. (Comparing the data in table 6-5 with those in table 6-4, we might say that as long as unit-sales volume is increasing by at least 6.7 percent, the firm might not need to raise its price when it makes mandatory investments—*all other factors held constant.*) The pro forma operating results, after we redefine the foregoing relation as $\Delta Q = C_I \Delta I$, are given by

$$\Delta(EBIT) = (C_I[P(1 - S) - U - V] - a - d)\Delta I,$$

$$\Delta(\text{Total assets}) = \left[C_I\left(\frac{PS + U + V}{t_c} + \frac{P}{t_a} + \frac{R}{t_r} + \frac{V}{t_i} \right) + \frac{a}{t_c} \right.$$

$$\left. + \frac{a + d}{t_i} + 1 \right]\Delta I,$$

$$\Delta(\text{Funds}) = \Delta(EBIT) - \Delta(\text{Total assets}) + d\Delta I/t_i.$$

Let us assume that our HMD is currently selling 18 million units. It is considering adding 10 percent to manufacturing facilities (in dollar terms)

Table 6-5
Incremental Volume Required by an Increase of 10 Percent in Fixed Investment for Manufacturing

Initial Volume (Millions)	Target-ROI Price	ΔQ(Millions)				Percentage Increase			
		a = 0	a = 0.1	a = 0.2	a = 0.3	a = 0	a = 0.1	a = 0.2	a = 0.3
2	$109.08	0.082	0.099	0.117	0.134	4.1	5.0	5.8	6.7
4	62.72	0.164	0.199	0.233	0.268				
6	47.32	0.246	0.298	0.350	0.402				
8	39.60	0.328	0.397	0.467	0.536				
10	34.97	0.410	0.497	0.583	0.670				
12	31.88	0.492	0.596	0.700	0.804				
14	29.67	0.575	0.696	0.817	0.938				
16	28.02	0.656	0.795	0.933	1.072				
18	26.73	0.739	0.894	1.050	1.206				
20	25.70	0.821	0.994	1.167	1.340	↓	↓	↓	↓

Note: $\Delta I = \$11.52$ million, $d = 0.1111$.

and expects, from either past experience or current projections, that cash fixed manufacturing costs will increase by $0.30 for each $1.00 increase in end-of-year fixed investment ($a = 0.3$). From table 6–5 we see that the firm must increase its unit-sales volume by 1.206 million units in order to maintain its 40-percent ROI. If it achieves this additional volume, then the pro forma results would show an incremental total investment of $26.329 million and an increase in operating profit of $10.086 million. Further, assuming a ten-year life and the same pattern of flows as assumed earlier, the investment yields an IRR of 27.31 percent. These data are summarized in table 6–6.

Investments in manufacturing fixed assets may be instrumental in reducing variable manufacturing costs. As far as financial theory is concerned, this category of investment would compete equally with investments to increase volume or revenue. However, the contemporary portfolio approach to strategic planning may place more emphasis on growth, cost reduction, or cash flow, depending on the principal mission of a division (for example, growth, maintenance, cash generation). The divisional mission becomes even more important when capital rationing is assumed—as it

Table 6–6
Pro Forma Pretax Funds Flow and After-Tax Internal Rate of Return Predicted by the 10-Percent Incremental Investment in Manufacturing Facilities

	Funds Flow		
Incremental returns			
EBIT		$10.086	
Depreciation		1.280	$11.366
Incremental investment			
Plant and equipment		$12.800	
Working capital			
Cash	$0.870		
Accounts receivable	8.059		
Raw materials	1.407		
Other inventory	3.103	13.439	26.239
Δ (funds)			($14.873)

	Internal Rate of Return					
Returns		6.726	6.726	. . .	6.726	13.439
Investment	12.8	13.439				
Year	0	1	2	. . .	10	11

Δ (Cash flow) = Δ(EBIT)(1 − *T*) + *d* Δ*I* = $6.726
     IRR = 27.33 percent

should be. Nevertheless, the basic approach to this class of investment is the same as to any other class, employing either DCF methods or the target-ROI approach.

Let us assume that the division is considering an investment designed to reduce other variable manufacturing costs (V'). A useful application of the target-ROI model is to determine the minimum reduction that will maintain the target ROI. This figure serves as the critical value, with no greater departure from DCF methods than those observed earlier in this chapter. The critical value, $\Delta V'$, is:

$$\Delta V' = -\left(\frac{a + d + K[a/t_c + (a + d)/t_i + 1]}{1 + K(/t_c + 1/t_i)}\right)\left(\frac{\Delta I}{Q}\right).$$

Note that assumed volume is a crucial element in cost-reduction investments. Our observation is that this is where most of the errors occur in capital-budgeting analysis for investments of this type, since the manufacturing group might have a tendency to assume a volume without consulting the marketing group.

As usual, it is convenient to reduce this relation to $\Delta V' = -C_I \Delta I / Q$, with C_I redefined previously. We can use this relation to work with either ΔV or ΔI. For instance, our HMD would show the following:

$$\Delta V' = -C_I \Delta I/Q = -0.774 \Delta I/Q,$$

as the 40-percent target-ROI criterion assuming that $a = 0.3$. The pro forma end-of-period operating results would then be

$$\Delta(\text{EBIT}) = (C_I - a - d)\Delta I,$$

$$\Delta(\text{Total assets}) = [(a - C_I)/t_c + (a + d - C_I)/t_i + 1]\Delta I.$$

As noted earlier, when inventory changes occur with no changes in volume, Δ (funds) needs special treatment. In this case, the reduction in inventory offsets the first period overstatement of operating profit; therefore, the change in funds from one equilibrium point to the next would be given by

$$\Delta(\text{Funds}) = [(C_I - a)(1 + 1/t_c) - (1 + d)]\Delta I.$$

From this relation, we can see that operating profit before depreciation is increased by $(C - a)\Delta I$, cash balances are reduced by $(C - a)\Delta/t_c$, and cash expenditures for the initial investment in fixed assets are $(1 + d)\Delta I$.

If a division's mission is to generate cash, then showing a target ROI or IRR on an investment to reduce manufacturing costs may be insufficient to obtain project acceptance, since external funding would still be required as long as the target ROI was within a realistic range. Thus, for a division manager in this situation the decision criterion may have to be $\Delta V'$, which yields a Δ(funds) greater than or equal to zero—implying that the reduction in other variable manufacturing costs is sufficient to pay off the investment with the increase in the division's own internally generated funds within the first year. In this case, the minimum reduction is

$$\Delta V' = -[(1 + d)/(1 + 1/t_c) + a]\Delta I/Q,$$

and the pro forma operating results would be defined as before where C_I is replaced by the foregoing term in brackets. As a boundary criterion, we might require that after-tax funds flow exceed zero. This would be defined by

$$\Delta V' = -\left(\frac{1 + d(1 - T)}{1 - T + 1/t_c} + a\right)\left(\frac{\Delta I}{Q}\right),$$

where T is the income-tax rate.

Obviously, another way to use these relations is to ask what investment would be required to yield a specific decrease in other variable manufacturing costs. This type of relation is illustrated in table 6–7. The table shows the beginning-of-period fixed investment, defined as $(1 + d)\Delta I$, required to achieve a \$0.30 reduction in other variable manufacturing costs (meaning a 10-percent reduction, since $V'_1 = \$3.00$ and $R = \$7.00$) for our HMD. The table assumes a ten-year depreciation period and illustrates both no fixed-cost increase ($a = 0$) and a large fixed-cost increase ($a = 0.3$). Each of the three decision criteria outlined here is illustrated. These data demonstrate what the HMD might be *willing* to spend on a 10-percent cost reduction.

Table 6–8 outlines the cost reductions required by a 10-percent increase in fixed manufacturing assets for our HMD, assuming a unit volume of 16 million and $a = 0.3$. Also illustrated are the pro forma operating results predicted by each decision criterion.

The ROIs and IRRs on the investments in table 6–8 are, in general, spectacular; but it is our observation that in mature divisions of large organizations, such requirements are quite common—managers just do not realize how confining the criteria are. For instance, for the Δ(funds) = 0 criterion in table 6–8, the after-tax payback period is 1.7 years (12.288/7.224). We have observed a payback criterion of 1.7 years being applied to mature divisions of one of the most financially successful conglomerates in the United States. For our HMD, the 1.7-year payback criterion yields an ROI of 125 percent and an internal rate of return (IRR) of 56.6 percent. Are the

Table 6–7
Investment in Fixed Assets Necessary to Achieve a 10-Percent Reduction in Other Variable Manufacturing Costs
(Millions)

	Required Fixed-Asset Expenditures		
Volume	K = 40 Percent	Δ (Funds) = 0	Δ (Funds)(After Tax) = 0
a = 0.3			
2	$ 0.861	$0.488	$0.314
4	1.722	0.976	0.628
6	2.583	1.463	0.942
8	3.445	1.951	1.256
10	4.306	2.439	1.571
12	5.167	2.927	1.885
14	6.028	3.415	2.199
16	6.889	3.902	2.513
18	7.750	4.390	3.827
20	8.611	4.878	3.141
a = 0			
2	$ 1.406	0.625	0.366
4	2.812	1.250	0.732
6	4.218	1.875	1.097
8	5.624	2.500	1.463
10	7.030	3.125	1.829
12	8.463	3.750	2.195
14	9.842	4.375	2.561
16	11.248	5.000	2.927
18	12.654	5.625	3.292
20	14.060	6.250	3.658

Note: $\Delta V' = \$0.30$.

prospects in other divisions that outstanding? Can other divisions yield an ROI exceeding 125 percent and an IRR above 56.6 percent? Since this example is imaginary, we cannot answer these questions; but we can conclude that these decision criteria are quite restrictive. At an extreme, one might say that such decision criteria may account for some of the deterioration of plant and equipment in U.S. industry.

The target-ROI model is also useful in decisions to invest in manufacturing facilities with a goal of reducing the per-unit cost of raw materials and purchased components. Since the basic method differs from investment

Table 6-8
Required Reduction in Other Variable Manufacturing Costs and Pro Forma Results for a 10-Percent Increase in Fixed Manufacturing Investment

	$K = 40$ Percent	Δ(Funds) = 0	Δ(Funds)(After Tax) = 0
Reduction in V'	$ 0.557	$ 0.984	$ 1.528
Δ (EBIT)[a]	$ 4.182	$ 11.008	$ 19.713
Depreciation	1.280	1.280	1.280
Pretax cash in	5.462	12.288	20.993
After-tax cash in	3.538	7.224	11.925
Investment in fixed assets	12.800	12.800	12.800
Decrease in working capital (cash)	0.228	0.512	0.875
Cash out	12.572	12.288	11.925
Δ (Funds)	(7.110)	0	9.068
Δ (Funds)(after tax)	(9.034)	(5.064)	0
Incremental ROI (percent)	40	125	294.1
IRR (percent)	25.1	56.6	93.3

Note: $\Delta I = \$11.52$ million, $Q = 16$ million, $a = 0.3$, $d = 0.1111$.
[a]Dollar amounts here and following in millions.

to reduce V' only by the effect on raw materials inventory, we need little introduction. When fixed investment increases by ΔI, the reduction in raw materials and purchased components, ΔR, required to maintain the target ROI is given by

$$\Delta R = -\left(\frac{a + d + K[a/t_c + (a + d)/t_i + 1]}{1 + K(1/t_c + 1/t_r + 1/t_i)}\right)\left(\frac{\Delta I}{Q}\right).$$

Table 6-9 illustrates this relation for our HMD, where we again assume a 10-percent increment in manufacturing facilities ($\Delta I = \$11.52$ million). The obvious and significant effect of estimated volume on the minimum decrease in R required to maintain the 40-percent target ROI is well illustrated in the table, as is the effect of increases in fixed manufacturing cost. The pro forma operating results outlined in table 6-9 are easily obtainable, again by reducing the change relation to $\Delta R = -C_I \Delta I/Q$.

Table 6–9

Minimum Reduction in per-Unit Cost of Raw Materials Required by a 10-Percent Increase in Manufacturing Investment

Volume (Millions)	a = 0			a = 0.3		
	− ΔR	Δ(EBIT) (Millions)	Δ(Funds) (Millions)	− ΔR	Δ(EBIT) (Millions)	Δ(Funds) (Millions)
2	$2.57	$3.87	($6.58)	$4.20	$3.67	($6.24)
4	1.29			2.10		
6	0.86			1.40		
8	0.64			1.05		
10	0.51			0.84		
12	0.43			0.70		
14	0.37			0.60		
16	0.32			0.53		
18	0.29			0.47		
20	0.26	↓	↓	0.42	↓	↓

Note: ΔI = $11.52 million, d = 0.1111.

$$\Delta(\text{EBIT}) = (C_I - a - d)\Delta I,$$

$$\Delta(\text{Total assets}) = \left(\frac{a - C_I}{t_c} - \frac{C_I}{t_r} + \frac{a + d - C_I}{t_i} + 1\right)\Delta I,$$

$$\Delta(\text{Funds}) = [C_I(1 + 1/t_c + 1/t_r) - a(1 + 1/t_c) - (1 + d)]\Delta I.$$

The fact that changes in operating profit, total assets, and funds requirements are independent of estimated volume is made explicit in these relations and is illustrated in table 6–9.

However, there may be a more fundamental decision for our HMD with respect to raw materials and purchased components. Since these costs amount to 70 percent of total variable manufacturing costs, the division might be much more troubled by the problem of securing long-term sources of supply than by the problem of simply reducing costs. This obviously leads to the classical make-or-buy decision.

For example, suppose our HMD could buy or build facilities to manufacture some of its purchased components at an end-of-period cost represented by ΔI. The fixed costs associated with operating the facility would be $ac\,\Delta I$, and in-house processing requirements would increase other variable manufacturing costs such as direct labor by $\Delta V'$. The manager would then want to know how much the per-unit cost of raw materials must decrease, assuming constant volume, in order to maintain the target ROI. Here, the building-block approach is again appropriate. The relation would be given by

$$\Delta R = \frac{(a + d + K[a/t_c + (a + d)/t_i + 1])\Delta I/Q + [1 + K(1/t_c + 1/t_i)]\Delta V'}{1 + K(1/t_c + 1/t_r + 1/t_i)}$$

The relation is used in the scenario pictured in table 6–10. The estimated cost of the proposed manufacturing facilities is \$25 million, with a twenty-year depreciation period. The fixed cost ratio is 30 percent, and other variable manufacturing costs will increase by an estimated \$2.00 per unit. The division's volume is expected to remain constant at 16 million units. In order to maintain its 40-percent target ROI, it must reduce the per-unit cost of purchased components by at least \$2.89. If it achieved this reduction, the incremental operating profit would be \$5.87 million and, if we estimate IRR by $K(1 - T)/[1 - K(1 - T)]$, the internal rate of return certainly would be in the range of acceptability.

This analysis, of course, does not lead inexorably to a decision to make rather than buy. The illustration is intended to demonstrate how the target-

Table 6–10
Illustration of a Make-or-Buy Decision Using the Target-ROI Model

---

Target ROI = 40 percent

Cost of manufacturing facilities = \$25 million

Fixed-cost proportion (a) = 30 percent

Increase in other variable manufacturing cost $(\Delta V')$ = \$2.00 per unit

Depreciation period = 20 years

Depreciation rate (d) = 0.05/0.95 = 0.0526

End-of-period investment (ΔI) = \$23.75 million

Estimated annual unit volume (Q) = 16 million

All turnovers and other costs in table 2–1

$$\Delta R = -\frac{|a + d + K[a/t_c + (a + d)/t_i + 1]|\Delta I/Q + [1 + K(1/t_c + 1/t_i)]\Delta V'}{1 + K(1/t_c + 1/t_r + 1/t_i)}$$

Δ(Variable manufacturing cost) = $\Delta V = \Delta V' + \Delta R = -\$0.89$

Δ(Average manufacturing cost) = $\Delta V + a\Delta I/Q = -\$0.44$

Δ(EBIT) = $-Q\Delta V - (a + d)\Delta I = \$5.87$ million

$$\Delta\text{(Total assets)} = \frac{Q\Delta V + a\Delta I}{t_c} + \frac{Q\Delta R}{t_r} + \frac{Q\Delta C + (a + d)\Delta I}{t_i} + \Delta I = \$14.57 \text{ million}$$

ROI method adds analytical information to such a decision. Where the actual decision is concerned, no quantitative model is sufficient to handle all the imponderables of make or buy. In our opinion, most quantitative models would lean in favor of the make alternative given the amounts of the cost reductions observed in table 6–10. Yet the real issues in manufacturing and technology policy are, first, ensuring a source of supply and, second, not locking oneself into a technology that may soon become obsolete.

Investments in fixed assets that are incurred to increase inventory turnover are another set of relations that are made explicit by the target-ROI method. Two concerns must be addressed, however, before the relations are presented. First, investment in, say, materials-handling equipment for finished goods may more appropriately affect selling expenses (U or F') than inventory turnover. Second, the allocation of such investment, for purposes of depreciation, to manufacturing or selling must be made prior to the use of the model. When these questions are resolved, the application of the target-ROI model is straightforward.

If a firm desires to increase its turnover of goods in process and finished goods by Δt_i, the maximum investment allowed in order to maintain the target ROI is given by

$$\Delta I = \left(\frac{K(QV + F + m_1 d_1 I_1)}{a + d + K[a/t_c + (a + m_2 d_2)/t_{i2} + 1]} \right) \left(\frac{\Delta t_i}{t_{i1} t_{i2}} \right).$$

where the proportion m_2 in the denominator would be set as a function of the allocation of the incremental investment to manufacturing ($m_2 = 1$), selling ($m_2 = 0$) or some combination of the two. For an increase in raw-materials turnover of Δt_r, the relation would be

$$\Delta I = \left(\frac{KQR}{a + d + K[a/t_c + (a + d)/t_i + 1]} \right) \left(\frac{\Delta t_r}{t_{r1} t_{r2}} \right),$$

since the allocation of $d \Delta I$ would certainly be to manufacturing.

Summary

DCF techniques rather than book-ROI criteria are the appropriate bases for analyzing capital expenditures, particularly at the corporate level. The target-ROI model yields a direct conversion to the IRR for investments in working capital under generally assumed conditions. The target-ROI model gives an approximation to the IRR, under some conditions, for investments in fixed assets; however, we do not recommend its use to the *exclusion* of DCF methods. The value of the ROI model in analyzing investments in fixed assets lies in its consideration of the short-term book effects of decisions, éffects that invariably influence the evaluations of divisional managers.

Note

1. Robert W. Williamson, "Measuring Divisional Profitability," *Management Accounting,* January 1975.

Appendix 6A
Alternative IRR
Calculation

This appendix considers an alternative way of calculating the internal rate of return for working-capital investment, and shows how the IRR might be derived differently, using the common technique for deriving cost of capital. In the long run, cost of capital and the IRR must coincide. Let r = cost of capital = internal rate of return, and K' = return on stockholder equity. Then,

$$r = K'(1 - D) + iD(1 - T),$$

where D, i, and T are the debt ratio, interest rate, and tax rate respectively. Chapter 1 showed that ROE in our model is given by

$$K' = \frac{G}{E(1 + G)}.$$

Then the IRR is

$$r = \frac{G(1 - D)}{E(1 + G)} + iD(1 - T).$$

ROI from chapter 1 is

$$K = \frac{G(1 - K)}{E(1 + G)(1 - T)} + iD$$

Because $K' = G/[E(1 + G)]$, we can substitute as follows.

$$K = \frac{K'(1 - D)}{1 - T} + iD.$$

Multiplying both sides by $(1 - T)$,

$$K(1 - T) = K'(1 - D) + iD(1 - T),$$

so that $K(1 - T)$ equals cost of capital and the IRR. This differs from our equation in the chapter because we assumed in the chapter that working-capital investment occurred at the end of the first year and was returned one year after the end of the life of the investment. If one wishes to assume that the investment in working capital occurs immediately (time zero) and is returned at the end of the life of the investment, then the IRR is $K(1 - T)$.

With respect to investments in fixed assets, we reiterate that our approximation to the IRR is just that: an approximation that one should not rely on in making large capital expenditures, but that does give a quick ballpark figure over a fairly wide range of possibilities for ROI and IRR.

Index

About the Authors

George E. Manners, Jr., Professor of Industrial Management, Clemson University. A former faculty member at Atlanta University, Georgia State University, the University of Notre Dame, and Rensselaer Polytechnic Institute, he came to Clemson in 1981. His professional interests are primarily the management of science and technology and strategic planning. He has served as a consultant to companies such as American Cyanamid, Colt Industries, General Electric, General Tire, IBM, and Philip Morris as well as such government agencies as NSF and DOE.

Joseph G. Louderback III., Associate Professor of Management, Rensselaer Polytechnic Institute. He has been a member of the Rensselaer faculty since 1977, having taught formerly at the State University of New York at Albany, Texas Christian University, and the University of Florida. A certified public accountant and auditor with Main, Lafrentz & Co. He is the author of several articles and textbooks in the finance and accounting field, including *Managerial Accounting* (Kent Publishing Co.), *Cost Accounting* (Kent Publishing Co.), and *Problems in Basic Business Finance* (Canfield Press).